STRANGERS AT THE DOOR

STRANGERS
AT THE DOOR

MARCUS BACH

Abingdon Press
Nashville and New York

STRANGERS AT THE DOOR

ISBN 0-687-39946-7

Library of Congress Catalog Card Number: 76-148064

SET UP, PRINTED, AND BOUND BY THE
PARTHENON   PRESS,   AT   NASHVILLE,
TENNESSEE, UNITED STATES OF AMERICA

Fondly Dedicated
to
Mabel Humphrey

CONTENTS

1
Strangers at the Door

1

It was inevitable. The day was bound to come when countries around the world to whom we had been sending missionaries would be sending missionaries to us.

This is the day.

From India, where Christianity traces back to the efforts of St. Thomas in A.D. 52, come gurus, swamis, and maharishis. From Indonesia, where Portuguese Catholics planted the cross in 1511 and where mass evangelism was hailed a triumph, come avatars and prophets intent on saving us from ourselves.

Out of the Land of the Rising Sun, where the Catholic Mass was introduced by Francis Xavier in 1549 and where Christianity-at-large had plans for wresting the islands from both the Kami and the Buddha, tides of new religions wash our shores bearing the persistent imprint "made in Japan."

The Near East, parental home of Christianity and first frontier for missionary efforts, sends us an accredited savior whose multi-million-dollar temple is a showplace in the American midwest. Out of China, target for conversion since Marco Polo colporteured Christian tracts to Kublai Khan in 1300, come master missioners of Tao and Zen with plans to guide us out of materialistic morass into quietude and peace.

The phenomenon is particularly unique because the newcomers are basically non-Christian, at best syncretic, and geared to chart a route between the western world's deep spiritual trauma and its religious discontent. The traditional church, floating in a world of new horizons, says with a shrug that it has always had its challengers. Until today, however, the contenders were spawned from within Christianity, rarely from such "pagan" sources as Hinduism, Islam, Buddhism, or from the spin-off groups of religions' "rabid left."

This makes the common encounter uncommon, and those who do not recognize this historic variant may be deceived into thinking it is just another innocuous reformation of the kind once posed by religions "made in the U.S.A.," groups like Mormonism, Christian Science, Spiritualism, Science of Mind, Unity, and other metaphysical movements.

"Schismatic sects and pretenders to the throne of Christian truth have always been around," a minister told me complacently. "We absorbed some and learned to live with others. They haven't really made much difference."

He was right, but this time he was also wrong.

2

As a young minister ambitiously serving my first congregation in a midwestern town, one of my earliest recollections was the sight of an avant garde of Pentecostals pitching their evangelistic tent in an open field within full range of my white-steepled church.

I can see them now. Five men and two youngsters of the local citizenry. Four strangers. I watch them as they yank the soggy folds of yellow canvas from a truck whose panels bear the ominous admonition, PREPARE TO MEET THY GOD, and on the tailgate in red and gold, JESUS SAVES.

I remember the sound of heavy hammers driving stakes into the autumn ground. I recall the disconcerting laughter of the workers as they heave the canvas toward the sky. I see the schoolchildren, curious as if a circus has come to town. I hear the ringing of the telephone on my study desk and the voice of the president of my church board saying, "It's all legal, their putting up the tent. There is nothing we can do. They'll only stay a week, but that means two Sundays. Do you have any plans?"

Did I have any plans? Did the early church have any plans, outside of excommunication, against the intrusion of the Montanists who believed in ecstatic visions and speaking in tongues? Did the church fathers have plans to hold off the Arians who taught that Christ was neither God nor man?

Did Catholicism have any plans to stop the Reformation? Did Luther have a program for restraining the rise of "sects," or did Wesley have a method for counteracting the growing flurry of schismatic groups? Did Congregationalism have any plans for stopping the threat of Unitarianism, or did the church-at-large contrive a way to resist Jehovah's Witnesses?

For that matter, did Roman Catholicism have a device for meeting the current theological and social revolution, or a scheme to silence Teilhard de Chardin, or a way to appease its errant priests? Did Protestantism have any plans for dealing with the underground church, or did institutionalized religion have a stratagem for saving itself from public demonstrations against war, injustice, racism, and the like?

The tent went up. For a long week my ministry was on trial. My dogmatic view that God could rightly be known and interpreted only by way of my traditional denomination was on the defensive. Sundays I tried to outpreach the evangelist while my congregation did its best to outsing his singers, so much so that it actually was a bit lonely when the tent came down and the intruders moved on to pitch their canvas top in other fields.

They never really left, however, for a remnant remained, a resolute band of dedicated believers who felt they had found something dynamic, who met in homes, then opened a storefront church and eventually built a "tabernacle" which they dedicated on the day of Pentecost with gospel hymns and glossolalic prayers.

3

In later years when my research took me across the world and I predicted that new faiths were preparing to migrate to America in search of us, I had the lingering feeling that religion, like Aristotle's theory of matter, can have now one form and now another of several substances in the form, while only the Creator remains aloof and formless.

Was it possible that religion, which is spiritual matter, embodied in itself countless expressions, emerging, multiplying, betraying some enchanted semblance of the formless God? God as Spirit became more clear to me when I lived with people of many faiths in many lands. I had a hunch that a rigid sectarianism, be it Evangelical or evangelistic or whatever, could never stand the test of either truth or time without a confrontation. And that was as it ought to be.

I remember the words of a medical practitioner in my parish who was my confidant in those days when the growing pains of spiritual ecumenicity got into my blood. He called the varieties of religious expressions "mitotic."

"The multiplication of cells is a manifestation of an inherent vital force," he assured me. "Eventually cells are created that are different from the parent cell. This is what happens in the growth of religious denominations, with the gametes seeing to it that hereditary characteristics are transmitted and yet allowing for change and newborn features just the same. Mitosis is life. You cannot stop it."

This was before the days of public knowledge about DNA or the popularization of phenotypes, or the pre-

sumption that life could be created in test tubes. Old
Doc Reynolds may not have had the language of our
time, but he never lacked persuasion when he said,

"In religion, as in cell life, there is a period of
augmentation, another of perfection, another of
decline and, finally, one of cessation. As long as vitality
can rely on chemical and physical agencies for building
up the system, these agencies tend to preservation, but
when life ceases they tend to destruction. Not because
the vital principle has not the power of resisting these
agencies, but because it can no longer turn them into
the channel for preserving the system. Now go back to
your preaching."

4

Tents are going up again today. Not evangelistic
tents. They are of the past. Not canvas tops, but
temples of steel and stone and, more significantly, temples of an expanding Self, reaching in, turning on, moving out in full view of Church Street, while we of the
established church still try to outpreach them and outsing them instead of investigating them—and ourselves
—as I did when the so-called American-born religions
elbowed their way into my fenced-off parish.

Mitotic division? A changing era? A new breed of
believers? Have the Christian faiths as we know them
grown old and impotent? Has the church really left *us*?
Has it become difficult for men to perceive the church's
mission, much less believe in it?

The "made in *America*" religions mentioned earlier,
new and on the march thirty years ago when I began
researching them, have leveled out and mellowed,

docilely taking their respectable places in faith's Establishment. It is no longer a spin-off group or an intrinsically Christian religion that confronts and challenges the traditional church. Defection from Christian ranks is due not only to schisms and the clash and change of theological and doctrinal views; the heart of the matter is that the philosophy presented by "foreign faiths" has caught the imagination and stimulated the thought of Americans to a degree beyond our willingness to admit. The void created by our social unrest, generation gaps, ideological change, the inability of institutionalized religion to provide persuasive answers to the intensification of our quest for truth, and most of all our failure to live the love that Christianity demands—these are providing fertile ground and fair game for these new off-shore groups.

Ironically, while the liberal trend is toward activism and involvement, and the conservative attitude re-emphasizes salvation as the watchword of belief, the appeal of the newcomers is toward self-awareness, spiritual identity, love, joy and peace with God here and now.

Against the full force of the argument that the church must become a politico-power-structure, the outlanders who have invaded Church Street ask primary loyalty to God as manifested in Self, confident that this kind of recognition will direct the individual wisely in his attitude in social and political concerns.

Yet, at that, the basic message of the strangers at our door is essentially the same as that of the indigenously American movements of several years ago. The ingredients are all here: unfoldment, security, inner awareness, belief in the miraculous, promises of rewards, techniques to live by and ideals to die for. The one area which the newcomers significantly avoid is the Christ-centeredness which has always been our Christian distinctive.

For this reason many Christian clerics feel justified in writing these groups off as heretical. No religion without Jesus can ever succeed, they say, and there, as far as they are concerned, the matter stands. It is tempting to agree with this point of view, but if there were some way we could examine the private beliefs of professed believers, if we had some psychic insight to get at the heart of things, we might discover more unrest, discontent, and confusion about him as a theological figure than we are willing to admit. He must be experienced to be believed. He must be lived to be understood. His love and teaching must be demonstrated in order to endure.

As theology has fashioned him and as our western culture has represented him, he is not truly inseparable from us in either our thoughts or acts. From the Savior with a bleeding heart whose agony disturbs us, to the Christ of the Ozarks who lends himself marvelously to marble as a tourist attraction, he has become an image which has too often taken on the mask of modern man.

So say the strangers at our door.

5

It was inevitable. Eventually the wheel of time turns to a confrontation with the past. This is not to say that our motivations were not sincere or that our missionaries were lacking in self-sacrifice. In my parental church we had a saying: "The zeal for foreign missions is the life-blood of the church." We supported missionaries we had never seen who converted people we had never known. No matter. The "Great Commission" had put us under orders to go into all the world and save the lost. Some say this is still the churches' chief assignment, but that is precisely how the new non-Christian religions feel about *their* great commission to mankind.

They are as sincere in their pioneering intentions as we were in ours; and there is as deep-rooted a conviction among them as there was among our missionary bands that the "gospel" must be preached in every nook and cranny of the earth. Our spiritual involvement was always global. Now theirs is, too.

They do not, however, have our apocalyptic vision; at least they do not make a point of it. They contend that the "kingdom" comes with a recognition of one's inherent oneness with God. They lay little stress on a "redemptive plan" or on credentials for "salvation." A man is saved, they say, when he knows that he is God particularized. They are less interested in labels and more aware of the ecumenicity of the spirit than we have been. They believe that time is on their side. Give or take another twenty years and denominationalism will be a thing of the past. Another fifty years and earthlings will be moving cooperatively in space. Another century and religions will share a universal approach in their deepening quest. By whatever sign we had hoped to conquer or survive as Christians, they have their signs as well: a Buddha, a Krishna, a Patanjali, a Nichiren, a Kobo Daishi, an Om or Prem or a

17

koan, a Buddhist triad, an ankh cross, a mantra. I hear them rapping at our door.

How did they originate? What do they believe? Where are they going? What have they to offer and by what presumption do they assume that we have failed? How shall we deal with them in their challenge and how seriously should we investigate their secret source of strength?

To discover in greater detail what they think of us and what we may rightly think of them, to let them speak for themselves and to allow us to do our thinking and form our own judgments, this may constitute for us a new and helpful adventure in the faith and challenge of our time.

2
The Art of Being

1

Some of my best friends are Vedantists. They have found their way into this eastern religion by many paths. Some moved quietly out of the traditional church in what they called a spiritual quest. They happened to read a book on Hinduism or to meet someone who had found something worthwhile in this ancient faith and decided to give it a try.

Other spiritual nomads, who had no official church connection, pricked up their ears when they heard a lecture on Vedanta or were thrilled when they came face to face with a personable Swami who impressed them with an uncanny insight into their particular seeking.

By far the greatest number simply became interested as part of their growth in what they considered a new step toward spiritual unfoldment. There was Vedanta, standing at the door waiting to be embraced as a practical system for meeting the challenges of modern life. Turning to it more and more, these spiritual nomads gradually realized an exceptional sense of at-homeness in the world.

There is really no mystery to all this. I came close to becoming a Vedantist myself. Its subtle overtones and enviable tradition dawned on me when I was first exposed to Gerald Heard. A companion and I slipped into a Vedanta temple in Los Angeles one Sunday morning some years ago, lured by a church-page-ad which had announced a lecture by this famous Cambridge graduate, who at the time was a science commentator on BBC.

My friend and I stood in the open doorway of the temple foyer, not only because the place was crowded and we were somewhat late, but by reason of the fact that if we did not like the lecture we could make a graceful get away.

Whiffs of fragrant incense drifted out to us from the flower-decked chancel where a youthful swami in ochre cassock was seated in quiet repose. A large portrait of a Hindu saint gave the chancel the semblance of a shrine. From the walls, pictures of Jesus, the Buddha, and other religious figures looked out at me as thoughtfully as I looked at them.

Mr. Heard, tall, slightly built, a profoundly engaging man, was addressing the congregation in scholarly style. Impressive by virtue of a well-trimmed beard, a healthy tan, and a casual yet dynamic way of speaking, he tantalized me to guess whether he was thirty or fifty, and whether his russet sports jacket and green slacks, as unconventional as Hollywood, were part of a plot to draw us closer into his fellowship. He stood before us as if he stood among us, as if he clearly saw something enthroned in each of us which we did not quite see. Before I knew it, the incense and the pictures and even the swami were ruled out, lost in the force and logic of Heard's compelling words.

As I think about it now, it was something more than his message that got through to me. Something charismatic. When he etched into my mind that, "Step by step we mount the spiral to the reality of God, the germ of our eternal life consuming the husk of our ego," that was dramatic enough, but there was the unmistakable evidence that he himself bore the magic of those who climb, often alone, always with a Presence, finding and feeling that Something which others so desperately seek.

"The spiral leads upward to the only Reality," I heard him say. "We rise from servanthood to friendship to Sonship. We rise through purgation. We rise into illumination and upward to creative purpose. The spiral leads from self-consciousness to union with the All, from self-love to love of God. Then our ego dies and we are born. We empty ourselves of self and the Spirit fills us."

Out of the hour-long session I remembered these and other phrases. I remembered the impact of Heard. We did not leave that service until the crowd began moving out, taking us along against our will. In fact, I never really left. My friend became a follower of Vedanta. I didn't. I found another way. My way. A way that gradually became more clear.

2

From that moment when Vedanta was first clearly sighted, I began familiarizing myself with it, wondering if this might really be for me, a questing Protestant, never quite fully satisfied with my parental faith. Soon I was involved with Vedanta's founder, a man with an overpowering name, Badarayana. Some authorities said he lived five hundred years before the time of Christ, but he was very much alive in the minds of Vedanta scholars. Whenever he lived and whoever he was, he took the Vedas, oldest of Hindu scriptures, dating back to 1200 B.C., and by way of study, reflection, and intuitive insight distilled out of these ancient texts some intriguing truths about God, the universe, and the soul of man.

What struck me was the *timeliness* of the things he found in these timeless writings. How could the unknown writers of the Vedas, or how could Badarayana, granted he was a mystic and even a saint, tell me what our modern world with all its scientific skills was just now beginning to discover: that matter is energy, that the universe is both knowable and transcendent, and that the deepest nature of God can never be completely fathomed by the human mind?

Why did all this strike me as so remarkable? Why did it intrigue those friends of mine who had become Vedantists? Why did it give them a greater sense of oneness and at-homeness in the world than they had found in their churches where, it was assumed, God cannot only *be* known, but intimately influenced and directed through the power of prayer?

Was it because our prayers so often failed to "work" as we thought they should? Was it because we had a feeling that even though we professed to know God, at our deepest feeling level we had a hunch we did not know him? Was it by reason of this fact that just when we felt we had God all neatly computerized and data-processed, he did not respond as we were sure he would? While we doggedly insisted that we *did* know him, something told us hauntingly that he was actually too big for us, or else we were too small for him. He often slipped away. Out of our reach. Beyond our grasp. Where are you, Father, now that we need you?

Paradoxically, it seemed that when we admitted, by way of Vedanta, that God remained essentially a mystery and that we could not ever really know him, then, all of a sudden, we knew him better than before.

Badarayana was a stranger and I let him in. I pictured him as an ascetic, a rishi, a quiet, reflective man, unrolling ancient scrolls, lost in wonder, devoting himself to the "last, thorough, comprehensive analysis of the Vedas" which is the meaning of Vedanta. Finding that God cannot be fathomed, Vedanta called God "Brahman," the Self-Existent, the Universal Spirit, the Ultimate Principle.

But if God could not be known, he could be perceived. In Hinduism, no less than in Christianity, a trinity had been formulated. Called the *Trimurti,* it consisted of *Brahma,* Vishnu, and Shiva. This trinity could be known through Brahman, the impersonal Reality, the Personification, who was sufficiently "human" to be loved and understood.

The words of Heard came back to me. "The spiral! We rise from servanthood to friendship, to Sonship. Our ego dies and we are born!"

When we make religion an adventure in spirit, it becomes a driving power in our lives. When we visit with the strangers at our door, we make our first immense discovery. What they are telling us we already knew, though for some reason we never knew we knew it.

For you see, when Vedanta assured me that while God cannot be known by logic or by the struggle of reason, while he cannot be fully entered into by the rational, reasoning, clever mind, he can be known by intuition, perception, inspiration, love. And when this dawned on me, my thoughts went deeply into India, but deeper still, they went to Galilee.

I remember how convincing Vedanta made its philosophical point when it said, "Intellect, which is part of the Integral man, cannot reach the Reality, which is the Whole. The entire consciousness must be concentrated upon the Ideal to be attained. The deeper the consciousness realized by an individual, the nearer it is to the Eternal."

I remembered how I memorized its statement of truth, "The object of thought can be known only when it is freed from the modes of thought, and the truth of thought can be known only when it is not conditioned by the form it takes."

And all the while something said to me, "You mean to tell me you had to find Vedanta in order to discover this? You mean that Jesus did not make this clear?"

Maybe he did. I'm sure he did. Maybe I missed it. I'm sure I did.

3

Tell me, Badarayana, what is new or distinctive in the process of finding God intuitively and by way of love?

"There is really nothing that is new," he seemed to say as if realizing the point of my question. "The Vedas were already old when Christ was born. They merely remind us that we get to know God by way of inner growth, though this truth is deeply couched in philosophical thought. The growth comes in many ways, through experience, insight, freedom, and most often out of fellowship with those who have developed the disposition and the nature to know. Growth comes from those who live close to the Personification of God and who are not deterred by the world or by false reasoning or illusion. It comes from those who serve for the sake of serving, who meditate for the joy of spiritual communion, who live and move in the light of love. It comes most of all from those who know that they are themselves the Personification. They, too, are Brahman. Vedanta has a saying, 'Yonder Person I am He.' "

As far as Badarayana was concerned and insofar as he interpreted the Vedic texts, that was the heart of it. Brahman was the way and, I added, with my own Champion of faith in mind, "the truth and the life." And I got to wondering whether, if Badarayana had lived in A.D. 500 instead of in 500 B.C., and if he had met the man who said, "Beloved, now are ye the chil-

25

dren of God," would Badarayana not have said to me, "Why, yes, I understand," even as I was saying to him, "Why, yes, I know"?

No matter. Badarayana was a pre-Christian image of myself discovering the Universal Spirit within me, finding the Self-Existent Self as I thought of Sonship and the spiral, trying to make them relevant for our time.

But why did I need Vedanta to activate my Christian faith? Old though its scriptures were, why did I interpret them in a contemporary light? Why hadn't I been doing this with the text and history of my Christian faith?

Had my parental religion become commonplace and static because of familiarity? Did my old friends weary me, and were my traditional beliefs too stereotyped and frozen in forms and too hermetically sealed in the institutions I knew so well? Was my church too socially activistic and its ministry too much of this world? If Badarayana intrigued me, why not St. Paul? If Brahman gave a new challenge to meditation, why not the Christ? If Gerald Heard implanted new points of inspiration in me, why could not any sincere and charismatic figure in *my* particular faith do the same?

Here was Vedanta, assuring its people that God is not exclusive, not denominationalistic, playing no favorites, imposing no limitations, simply wanting a person to be, to know, to accept the fact that he and God are inseparably One.

Heavens! Why did anyone have to become a Vedantist when all Vedanta actually did was undergird the basic philosophy and ethics of the Christ!

For wasn't this what Jesus had been telling us? God

is God. His will may not always be your will. His ways are not always your ways. He is knowable but also transcendent, unknowable to the finite mind.

If God can be known only by logic, he is definitely God of the logicians. If only by theology, he is exclusively a theologian's God. If you must be wise to know him or ignorant to know him, or rich or poor or white or brown or young or old or short or tall or Christian or non-Christian to know him, he is not truly universal. But if he is God of life, then all and everything that lives is God in his expression, and so are you, and so am I.

Vedanta had a word for this all-inclusive soul or life of God. It called it *Atman,* and defined it as the ultimate Self of which all individual selves are the manifestation. When my friend became a Vedantist, he put great stress on Atman and explained it as the breath of life. Often when he took a deep inhalation he reminded himself that Atman sustained him and that, in the very act of breathing, God was continually being renewed and known. And why hadn't Christianity ever told him that?

And why hadn't I ever thought of it in that way? Strange. Even in my parental German home a great deal was made of the *Atem,* meaning the breath of God which, my Christian parents firmly assured me, had been breathed into me and into all mankind by the Maker of heaven and earth.

Vedanta was surely worthy of study, not because it led me only to Vedanta, but more and more because it seemed to lead me home.

4

Three inclusions in Vedanta fascinated me from the very start. They fascinate me still: Nondualism, Reincarnation, Karma. Each held convincing answers to many unanswered questions and all raised new questions for which apparently there were no answers, unless one settled things simply by saying, "I believe."

Nondualism, Reincarnation, Karma. I remember how some of us during our college work looked for enlightenment on these three concepts. We were told it would be necessary first to define our epistemological position. We were reminded that theology, divided into many disciplines, needed to approach each subject from the standpoint of its particular dogma, exegetic standard, hermeneutics, and other systematic preoccupations. Obviously such a process necessitated interminable sessions of jurisdictional procedure. So many sessions, in fact, that the cases deteriorated in the webs of time. In fact, this is exactly what happened to our three defendants (Nondualism, Reincarnation, Karma) when they were confronted by the polemics of the early church. They were thrown out of the Christian court.

But every once in a while they cropped up again to be tried by thoughtful jurists tantalized by their guilt or innocence. In the persistent testimony in their behalf, no stronger or more courageous witness had appeared than Hinduism, and Vedanta had been their most persuasive advocate.

Advaitist Vedanta's nondualism, the theory that "since God (Brahman) is One, there can be no plurality, because other than God nothing can be," was surely nothing new to the average non-Hindu believer. I grew up on its Christian counterpart: "God is all, and all is God." What I learned rather quickly and somewhat painfully about our Christian nondualism, however, was that we needed a dualistic support in order to explain and justify our nondualism. God was all, but there was also evil in the world. All was God, but there was also sin lurking around. God was all and all was God, but things were often in an ungodly mess in the world that God had made.

So we summoned a new dualism to the rescue. We pointed out that there were two forces at work in the universe, Logos and Lucifer, good angels and bad, mind and matter, God-stuff and world-stuff, and anyone with half an eye could see that these were always two. One God there surely was and one reality, but the positive and negative features could not be denied. When I would do good, evil *was* present with me, and I knew this fully as well as Paul.

Along came Vedanta with a new idea, for me at least, and a new word. It maintained that the reason we see God not as One but as many and the reason we construe apparent evil as evil is because the world, the mind, and the thoughts of man are shrouded by *maya*. That was the new word: *maya,* a veiling or an obscuring force of nature which gives the *impression* of duality and produces all sorts of illusions and phenomena which appear to be real but are not, really. *Maya* was real only as a psychchosomatic sickness is real, or as a mirage is real.

Maya was descriptive of mirages of the mind, concepts built up in consciousness as though they were absolutely things of substance but were actually Brahman, or God, disguised. The danger I thought was lurking in my life wasn't a danger but a blessing: the evil that turned out to be an adventure in experience. The worry that had no substance in fact. Chance that turned out to be divine design. *Maya.*

Vedanta, of course, was considerably more profound about all of this as I learned when, after my interest in Badarayana, I encountered Shankara, the eighth century figure said to have been the father of the doctrine of nondualism. Shankara saw *maya* as the great deceiver. It created forms in the formless, that is, it made God appear as if he were not one but many, beguiling people into seeing differences in nature instead of likeness. It worked a sinister magic causing men to insist that the unreal is the real, that the world as we see it and as it plays upon our senses is the true world, when in reality it is merely the gross world of illusion.

Addiction to *maya,* thinking in terms of duality, said Shankara, is a matter of plain stupidity. It is like fearing a rope because you imagine it to be a snake. In fact, it is not even a rope but God, expressed in form, behind which there is always his immutable nonform, and to those who have truly caught on to the theory of nondualism, the formless God is seen. A rope, a snake, water or a mirage, all are fleeting and descriptive forms only. The real God, said Shankara, is never affected or changed by the unreal.

Then came the giant leap into spiritual understanding: to know the Real is to realize you are the Real! Not the "you" I refer to when I say I am Marcus Bach.

30

Marcus Bach is not the Real. The Real is the *I* who says, "You are Marcus Bach!" The Real is the "I Am" who is the subject speaking of an object. The leap had to be made by way of faith and intuition, and when for a moment I made it, I discovered a basic Vedanta truth: faith and intuition are but the wings of ultimate logic and pure reason.

Now the paradoxical saying of Shankara became clear, "The Absolute can be realized only through knowledge and knowledge alone. In other words, knowledge confesses its ineptitude to know God and dies, only to become alive in God's knowing and live."

I remember the day the Real became real. I was standing at a window with a book on Shankara's Vedanta in my hands. I remember the sense of awakening that came to me, the thrill that ran through me when I looked out at old familiar scenes and saw the trees, the lane, and the sky not merely as manifestations of God, but as God in fact, and in that moment of unmistakable transformation, God and I were one. I stood there seeing the unseen through moist eyes and a deeply longing heart, wondering whether others in the world had felt what I was feeling and, if they had, what a world of peace this world would be. I remember how, just then, I was blessing Vedanta, thanking Shankara, and loving all mankind.

Then a thought came to me. Hadn't I *always* been taught that the things that are seen are made of things not seen? Wasn't it a traditional part of my Christian teaching that the physical world is not the real and that this cannot be grasped by an intellectual study but only by an inner, spiritual apprehension? What was *maya* but another word for the ignorance Christ talked about when he said in effect that a man who could not see beyond the phenomenal world was spiritually blind?

When I thought of this, I was no longer holding a book on Vedanta, for the moment I was once more in possession of the Christian revelation that God has made of one substance (himself) all manner of things that dwell on earth. He is the universe and the consciousness of man; his substance is the one and only true reality. The window at which I stood was suddenly filled with the momentary wonder of Christ's words that, "I and the Father are one."

5

If I was fascinated with nondualism it was hardly to be compared to my excitement about Hinduism's doctrine of reincarnation. The suggestion that we might conceivably have lived before, prior to this life, had, of course, long been a subject for tongue-in-cheek speculation by Christian scholars. A professor of mine had called it the "world's most damnable heresy," an opinion which he ruefully admitted put him in agreement with Roman Catholicism on as least one point, for the Catholic Church had cursed the teaching in its Ecumenical Council in A.D. 553 under Emperor Justinian. But now reincarnation was back at my door audaciously tapping for attention. Could it be, I wondered, that if the nondualistic theory was correct, it was my Self that stood there? Were the Vedanta philosophers right when they said,

"The food-formed vesture is merely the body. The true Self was before birth or death, and now is. It is of another nature than the body. Of this compound of skin, flesh, fat, bone and water, the man of deluded mind thinks, THIS IS I! But he who is possessed of judgment knows that his true Self is of other character. It is nature transcendental. Therefore, O thou of mind deluded, put away the thought that this *body* is the Self. Discern the *universal* Self, the Eternal, changeless, and enjoy supreme and everlasting peace."

It was not an easy stranger to entertain, this reincarnated Self. In the first place I remembered nothing about it; any recollection of a previous existence was hazy at best. Secondly, I was sure I would have been doing more this present life had I been in this classroom of physicality before. Thirdly, why would the soul want to come around again for another rebirth if its previous time around had been distasteful? And finally, although I had been hearing about reincarnation all my life, the threatening shadows of my clerical forebears stood over me scowling at the thought that I might ever take the theory seriously. I could have my speculations about purgatory if I wished, and even hazard some guesses about the Witch of Endor, but when it came to Hinduism and its heathen hint of rebirth and transmigration, there they drew the line.

Now there was Heard. And Aldous Huxley whom I got to know and respect. There was Swami Prabhavananda, founder of the Vedanta Society of Southern California, whose saintly nature had influenced secret idols of mine like Christopher Isherwood and playwright John Van Druten, and there were Vedantists who, because of a new sense of the continuity of life, had an enviable sense of equilibrium and a timeless touch in their at-homeness in the world. They seemed as if they actually had been here before. For countless eons they had never really left off living, excepting for brief vacation periods from physicality by way of the *maya*-inspired-phenomenon called death.

Here was Vedanta, quietly and in scholarly fashion making a case for reincarnation. Not actually a case, however, for it had long ago accepted it with the same believability that most Christians accepted the fact that the soul was made anew specifically for each body and each body for the soul.

As I think about it now, it was Vedanta's grand assumption rather than any solid proof that first drew me to a serious consideration of the reincarnation theory. The idea was simply so incredible that it dared me to investigate it. It held the same fascination for me that was evoked by suggestions such as, "It is possible to send words around the globe without the use of wires," or "Who ever believed we'd have television?" or "Someday everyone will have to believe in interplanetary travel," or "Who ever doubted there would be heart transplants?" In other words, now that nothing was any longer preposterous, why shouldn't we take another look at the theory that the life essence is capable of using first one body as its vehicle and then another?

There was a time I would have dismissed this on the ground that my church said it simply couldn't be. But there had been other things my church had told me simply couldn't be. The ageless age of the earth, for example. That the world was not created in six days of twenty-four hours each. That the infallible Bible is not necessarily the King James Version! That Catholics and Protestants could never get together, for example. The thought that beliefs would never change, beliefs about baptism, ethical codes, evolution, redemption, salvation, heaven, hell, the end of the world, the Second Coming, and priestly celibacy, for example. And so on.

What helped me most was the rising interest in reincarnation among the younger clergy of the church-at-large, a trend pinpointed by a noted clergyman not so young. In 1957 the psychologist-preacher-researcher-teacher, Leslie D. Weatherhead, titled his sermon in City Temple, London, "The Case for Reincarnation."

"If every birth in the world is the birth of a new soul," he said, "I don't see how progress can ever be consummated. Then each soul has to begin from scratch. How then can there be progress in the inner-most things of the heart? How can a world progress in inner things, which are the most important, if the birth of every new generation fills the world with un-regenerate souls full of original sin? There can never be a perfect world unless, gradually, those born into it can take advantage of lessons learned in earlier lives."

Hard on the heels of this manifesto which immedi-ately prompted ministers to speak more boldly on the subject, an anthology appeared titled *Reincarnation*. Editors Cranston and Head mobilized such an array of testimony in this Julian Press publication that it im-mediately became a standard text for anyone who needed authoritarian support for his hope or hunch that the doctrine of metempsychosis could conceivably be true.

Thomas Huxley was there saying, "Like the doctrine of evolution itself, that of reincarnation has its roots in the world of reality. None but very hasty thinkers will reject it on the grounds of inherent absurdity." Albert Schweitzer admitted that, "The idea of reincarnation contains a most comforting explanation of reality by means of which Indian thought surmounts difficulties which baffle the thinkers of Europe." Thomas Edison was quoted, "The only survival after death I can conceive of is to start a new earth cycle again." Philosophers were quoted, including Arthur Schopenhauer: "Were an Asiatic to ask me for a definition of Europe, I would be forced to answer him that it is that part of the world which is haunted by the incredible delusion that man was created out of nothing, and that his present birth is his first entrance into life." Psychiatrists and psychoanalysts had their say, among them Ian Stevenson, "Further investigation of apparent memories of former incarnations may well establish reincarnation as the most probable explanation of these experiences."

The testimonies included people of all creeds, councils of all major religions, citizens of all nations, scientists, poets, writers of all countries, not excluding voices of faith speaking from the atheistic laboratory of the USSR. "In me," Anton Chekhov was quoted as saying, "is the soul of Alexander the Great, of Caesar, of Shakespeare and of Napoleon, and of the lowest leech. In me the consciousness of man is blended with the instincts of the animals, and I remember all!"

While this may have been going further than Vedanta would possibly have gone, the fact remained, as far as I was concerned, that reincarnation was an hypothesis worthy of consideration. While it could not be "proved," neither could the single-cycle theory. Roughly speaking, half of the people in the world believed in reincarnation and half did not. For those who needed to settle for an absolute it was again a matter of believability, awareness, conviction, and dogged faith.

My way was different. I saw the entire matter as a quest, no matter which conclusion a man arrived at. The compatability was not only the insatiable search for the unknown, but it was also a stubborn determination to believe in some sort of immortality. The ancient saying was underlined, "If immortality is untrue, it matters little if anything else is true or not." My way was the search and the recognition that the search itself was the answer. This was part of the glory, and Vedanta seemed kind enough and gentle enough to appreciate my point of view. So, it seemed to me, did Jesus. For when he asked his disciples, "Whom do men say that I, the Son of man, am?" they said, "Some say that thou art John the Baptist, some, Elias, and others, Jeremias, or one of the prophets." And once he said of John the Baptist, "If ye will receive it, this is Elias, which was for to come. He that hath ears to hear, let him hear."

According to my way, the most remarkable verdict in the case for reincarnation was simply this: if there is anything to rebirth, then we who are living here and now on planet Earth have all gone through the immortal cycle previously. We have experienced life and death, earth and heaven many times, endless times, and it wasn't so bad. It was ever the great adventure. If, in order to reach that state of Nirvana, that union with God or Brahman, it was necessary for us to pass in and out of this classroom of life endless times, well and good. And it was an interesting thought to feel that, though we did not fully remember, we *had* been eyewitnesses and participants in the unfolding story of history in all ages, in all times, in all places, and we would be eyewitnesses again to the events that lay ahead in the ages yet to come.

6

Then there was Karma.

Vedanta explained Karma as the principle of causality, based on the concept that for every action there is a reaction. Reincarnation is regarded as a doctrine, Karma as a law. You can take reincarnation as fact or fancy, but you must accept Karma as a basic truth, for it is part of the immutable cosmic plan.

Here again the stranger was not so strange. My earliest catechetical instruction had impressed me with the Christian axiom that "as a man sows so shall he reap." The words had been part of my Judeo-Christian code, along with the Ten Commandments and the Apostle's Creed. They were gospel, uniting the Old and New Testaments and the church into a solid causal package. That they sounded more ominous than friendly was no doubt the fault of my wretched conscience. I was apparently always doing less than my

Christian best and falling somewhat short in my ability to run the Christian race.

One thing that the "as you sow" statement of the Christ certainly never did was to suggest that some of the crops I was reaping in this present life were the result of seeds sown in a pre-life or that what I planted in this life might bear their fruit in another earth journey after death. This was the most obvious difference between Vedanta's causal law and mine.

There was something else. Karma put the responsibility for my "salvation" squarely upon me. Not upon a minister. Not upon a priest. Not upon a plea for mercy. Not upon a promise to change my attitude. Not even upon a Savior. Yet in a way it did, for when I found my true Self I found both the object and the nature of the Savior, mercy and spiritual change.

The responsibility, according to Vedanta, was mine, and this seemed fair enough. There was no capricious law in which I was involved, nor was it one that played favorites, condemning some and blessing others.

But what happened, then, to my "personal Lord"? I missed him. I missed the love and charm and intimacy of "our Father." I missed the warm companionship of the Christ who, I was assured, was with me all the way. I had a sense of loss about him who, as the old songs assured me, "walks with me and talks with me and tells me I am his own." You don't—or at least I didn't—find quite this kind of feeling in either the Ultimate Principle or the Atman or in the Karmic law, nor even in the discovery that Yonder Person I Am He.

My Vedanta friends were convinced I had not gone deeply and wisely enough into the teachings, and I had no doubt that they were right. Things are not the same seen from the outside in as they are seen from the inside out. But I will say that Karma helped clear up any number of doubts about God's justice, and I have a hunch I believe in the causal law a bit more strongly today than even many Hindus do.

The "Karmic cycle" became and remains a breakthrough for me. I believe it more now than ever. It has given Christ's "as you sow" the horizon it needs for absolute believability. The Christian faith has been short-sighted in confining Karma to this life alone or relating Karma to the progressiveness of sin—and blessings—unto the third and fourth generations.

Cycles of birth and rebirth *are* involved in our life or lives, however you wish to construe them, and reading Vedanta carefully it is apparent that it also recognizes and anticipates the Christian "redemptive plan of grace." For in Vedanta man's true and highest good is something beyond his own power of attainment, true righteousness, if I may use the word, true identity with Atman. True salvation is a gift, a gift of the grace of understanding which cannot be earned through arduous labor. I began to feel about Karma as Emerson stated in his poem on Brahman,

> They reckon ill who leave me out;
> When me they fly, I am the wings;
> I am the doubter and the doubt,
> And I the hymn the Brahmin sings.

Karma was on the march and on people's minds. If a man believed in reincarnation, naturally he had to believe in Karma.

The New Thoughtists, the Theosophists, the Rosicrucians—even the Unity School of Christianity—were supporting the strangers Reincarnation and Karma when they came rapping at the door.

"Those who believe in Karma," said authoress Blavatsky, "have to believe in a destiny which, from birth to death, every man is weaving, thread by thread, around himself, as a spider does his web. Karma creates nothing, nor does it design anything. It is man who plants and creates causes, and Karmic law adjusts the effects, whose judgment is not an act but a universal harmony, tending ever to resume its original position, like a bough, which, bent down too forcibly, rebounds with corresponding vigor."

As in the case of reincarnation, so with Karma. Who could prove it absolutely? We could make our inferences, but even Vedanta was quick to point out that inferences do not change reality. We could say that some of our sufferings and blessings are the result of our individual acts in this or in some previous existence, but is this true of all our rewards? Does every era have its "Bridge of San Luis Rey" Are souls and spirits always involved with each other in the endless cycles of rebirth? On the other hand, if God ordains that some individuals should suffer or be blessed through no merit of their own, does this not involve him in injustice? Or is the "law of Karma" itself a masterly inference to explain the apparent injustices which have always defied our absolute faith in the goodness and mercy of God?

Always there was Karma.

And there was Ramakrishna.

Had I lived in India in the mid-1800s I would very likely have made my way to the village of Dakshineswar to meet Sri Ramakrishna, for he was said by many to be a holy man. No doubt I would have agreed with those who believed he had spiritual insights, that though he was married he lived a celibate life, and that he spoke words of wisdom and had an inner charismatic charm. Today there are those who insist that of all Hindu masters he was the greatest, and that without him Vedanta might never have been brought to the western world.

One thing was sure, he had proved an intriguing theory: it is possible to find self-realization in its highest form via many paths. He claimed he had found it by way of Hinduism, Judaism, Islam, Christianity, no less than through the spiritual discipline of other world religions which he apparently understood in their deepest mystical senses.

How did he know they all led to the same divine Reality? He had followed each one through to a state of superconsciousness and absolute emancipation, an experience Hinduism calls *samadhi*. It was like reaching the top of the Himalayas by many trails or arriving at the ocean, borne by the current of many streams.

This is how it happened in the Christian sense. One day Ramakrishna gazed intently at a picture of the Madonna and Child, reflecting on the life of Christ. The figures seemed to come alive. The Holy Mother was no longer the Divine Mother of Hinduism, she was

Mary, Queen of Heaven. The Child was not Brahman, it was the Christ. He felt his Hindu convictions literally pushed out of his life, and in desperation he cried out for help to the Hindu gods. "What are you doing to me?" he implored. "What is happening to me?"

Mary and Jesus filled his mind, his heart, his spirit. To quote his biographers, "His love and regard for the Hindu deities were swept away by this tidal wave, and in their stead a deep regard for Christ and the Christian Church possessed him. For three days visions of Christian devotees burning incense and candles before the figure of Jesus possessed him. On the fourth day, as he was walking in the Panchavati, he saw an extraordinary-looking person of serene aspect approaching him with a gaze fixed intently upon him. He knew him at once to be a man of foreign extraction. The figure drew near, and from the inmost recesses of Sri Ramakrishna's heart there went up the note: " 'This is Christ who poured out his heart's blood for the redemption of mankind and suffers for its sake. This is none else but the Master-Yogi Jesus, the embodiment of Love.' Then the Son of Man embraced Sri Ramakrishna and became merged in him. At this the Master went into Samadhi and lost all outward consciousness. Thus was Sri Ramakrishna convinced that Jesus Christ was an Incarnation of the Lord."

And since he experienced this with other avatars and had found his way to "heaven" and "salvation" no matter which major highway he took, I would have appreciated meeting him to see for myself how the light of God showed through his life and whether, perhaps, he was more compassionate and sensitive and empathic than those who insist there is one door and one alone which brings a pilgrim to that great white throne. For I have always had a notion that all roads that lead to God are good and that, as Teilhard de Chardin so beautifully said, "The more we pulverize matter, the more we discover its essential unity."

Actually I did go to Dakshineswar three quarters of a century after Ramakrishna entered *mahasamadhi,* which is death—and life. His passing was in 1886 and he was fifty. But when I was there the love for him among the Ramakrishna monks was as fresh and expressive as if he were in a corner of the ashram saying his prayers. And perhaps he was.

As for the history of Vedanta, it does seem to have been written in his name as far as America is concerned. All of the great swamis go back to Ramakrishna, and most of Ramakrishna's swamis have points of greatness. Brilliant, educated men, men of deep compassion and a kind of purity of mind, they came to the western world with the adage, "When the disciple is ready, the Master appears." One of the most persuasive was Ramakrishna's well-beloved Swami Vivekananda whose name I ran into when I was working in the Newberry Library doing research on phases of the Columbian Exposition.

The name had a good sound: Vivekananda. *Viveka* (pure discrimination); *Ananda* (pure bliss and also the blessed one). His words, with which he had introduced Vedanta to America at the Parliament of Religions in 1893, caught my eye, held me fast, made me wonder about my own faith. "Do I wish that the Hindu or Buddhist would become Christian? God forbid. The seed is put in the ground, and earth and air and water are placed around it. Does the seed become earth or air or water? No! It becomes a plant; it develops after the law of its own growth, assimilates the air, the earth and the water, converts them into plant substance and grows a plant. . . . If anybody dreams of the exclusive survival of his own religion and the destruction of others, I pity him from the bottom of my heart and point out to him that on the banner of every religion will soon be written, in spite of his resistance: *Help and not fight, assimilation and not destruction, harmony and peace and not dissension.*"

Vivekananda waylaid me. For several days my research on the Exposition took second place while I followed the princely swami on his continental tour. He spoke in churches, Unitarian and Universalist mostly, at service clubs, to women's groups, and on college campuses. Reporters followed him. Devotees lionized him. Ministers tried to discover the secret of his prophetic insight. His English was flawless. His voice was described as being "melodious as the sound of a harp." He spoke in parables, beatitudes, and in the messianic manner of his master Ramakrishna, who said, "God is in all men, but all men are not in God, and that is the reason for suffering!"

I wrote about him in one of my earliest books *(Faith and My Friends)* in which I tried to visualize what India's first formidable missionary to America was like. I said, "Chicagoans saw him in dazzling cassocks and silken turbans. But when his funds ran out they found him begging in the streets. In the lobbies of the best hotels he enjoyed the attention of wealthy women. In the city's slums he liked being with the poor. He was a mixture of calculated wisdom and simple piety, a man of universal knowledge and guileless mind, a master of possessive calm and a slave to emotion. He was both a mystic and a willing recipient of the riches and comfort of the wealthy. A Hindu who loved Christ. A contemplative who enjoyed society. An apostle of contradictions who trained himself to embrace the world in order to persuade others to embrace heaven."

Badarayana, Shankara, Ramakrishna! Nondualism, Reincarnation, Karma! Brahman, Brahma, Self! Vedanta was the belief that every soul is a circle whose circumference is nowhere and everywhere. It was a point of view that all religions are dialects by which man speaks to God and God to man. It had supreme confidence in the rightness of its views and in the soundness of its knowing. It believed that other faiths, all faiths, had appropriated many of its teachings and benefited from its insights, and paid respect to its vision of existence.

It has always been a closely knit fellowship, a sort of soul-ship consciousness of those who have been drawn by the magnetic pull of Vedanta masters. Behind its apparent simplicity and deceptive childlike naivete lurk vast reaches of cultivated wisdom. Swamis, teachers of enlightenment, give the impression of having seen the unseen and found it good. Death for them is an experience to be entered into philosophically. A terminal sickness, as one of the followers told me, was something to be observed and studied with the fascination of a mother watching the unfoldment of her growing child.

Self-unfoldment, Self-discovery were key words inspiring the building of temples and meditation centers in America's large metropolitan areas. I visited many of these centers and still do, never without reward and always to the enrichment of my own particular way of faith which has much in common, warm respect, and a friendly feeling for these no-longer-strangers at our door.

For I have never forgotten that once, long ago, when I heard of the spiral, which is a symbol for the ever-ascending quest, I came close to becoming a Vedantist and might indeed have done so but for the fact that, even at the time, I was already on another path.

3
Faith, Fun and Fitness

1

He came to me while I was teaching at the State University of Iowa. Pleasantly dark-skinned and slender of body, he regarded me as if I were a focal point in the universe, as if in his steady, smiling appraisal of me he was reading what I thought of him. Casually wrapped in a faded saffron-colored robe beneath which worn-out sandals unashamedly protruded, he was a picture of happy health. Brown eyes, soft and steady, mirrored his moods. He sat relaxed, hands clasped in his lap as if he had been born for this moment, in the right place at the right time, and all was well. But, then, he was young. In his mid-twenties. Too young almost for me to address him by his rightful title, *Swami*. But I did.

"Swami," I said, "let's call this meeting in my home your introduction to America, and tomorrow in the classroom let's say it will be my students' introduction to yoga and to you."

"Very good," he said, and I realized again that his relaxed attitude was a cover-up for a coil of steel spring that sprang into action the moment he spoke, for his words were rapid and impassioned.

"Why not?" he exclaimed. "God *does* these things. He led me from India to Australia and from Australia here. At a college in Australia I met Professor Hew Roberts. He said, "When you get to the United States, look up Marcus Bach." So here I am. You *don't* think things *happen* like this? Sure you do. I know you do or you would not be teaching religion. I can feel that you know things happen this way."

He kicked off his sandals, pulled his legs up under his robe and sat crosslegged on the overstuffed chair. Like a Buddha. Quietly and without pretension. Nothing he did was incongruous. It seemed the thing to do for him to sit this way and I liked him for it, but mostly for the charismatic presence he brought into the room and the softness of his nature which so artfully concealed his depth of strength.

Speaking of feeling things, my students quickly caught his charisma when he appeared in my classes. Iowa University's first skirmish with a swami was definitely a victory for two hundred and fifty young people enrolled in a course titled, "Little-known Religious Groups."

Several faculty members, even some in the department of religion, accused me of stretching academic freedom to a breaking point, especially since my students began intoning Om and Shanti and quoted Swami

Vishnudevananda to their professor. Vishnudevananda, the name itself, amused some administrative officials and caused concern among several of the local clergy. Literally translated, "blessed of the deity Vishnu," it was a bit too much, and discredited him in the eyes of those who were convinced that any Hindu regardless of name or title stood in need of being "saved."

The year of Swami's advent was 1958. As I think about it now, students on campus in those days were already generating the subtle power of a quest which was soon to take on seductive polarizations: anti-draft, anti-preconditioned thinking, anti-war, anti-racism, anti-academic authoritarianism. But Vishnudevananda apparently saw no evil, heard no evil, and spoke no evil, though he was looked down upon through ever-widening chinks in the ivory towers.

In his month-long stay with me, he alerted students to the need for personal discipline, which had a scientific rather than a mere dogmatic basis, as the Hatha Yoga he demonstrated clearly proved. He convinced us by virtue of his yogic prowess and the impelling force of his personality that the old masters of the East were ahead of us in their search for techniques for daily living and that they were still walking and talking with us, if only we took time to walk and talk with them. Flashes of revolt across new horizons of the inner man and outer space in those days fit into the Hatha Yoga system perfectly.

Pinpoint "miracles" happened wherever Swami went. When I took him to other campuses, to service clubs and to church assemblies, remarkable changes took place in aspiring adepts. Wherever yoga was seriously studied and practiced, no matter how elementarily, new frontiers immediately opened. Wherever Swami's teaching was faithfully pursued, old things literally passed away. In outlook, in concept of health and well-being, a new awareness and a new philosophy vividly transformed the individual life.

A student in one of my classes had been a chain smoker. He had dared me to prescribe a remedy or a reason why he should quit. He simply liked to smoke better than he liked to do anything else, and he used to expand his chest and flex his muscular body and say, "It isn't hurting *me!*" Swami's soft approach, his coil of boundless energy, the impact of his convictions about the body being the temple of God (which I had stressed to this young man without success) so captivated my cigarette-infatuated student that he quit the habit cold. He quit because he found something he would rather do than smoke: yogic breathing and yogic disciplines.

In short, I saw the beginning of a new religion that is really not a religion, and the start of a movement which now has American headquarters in New York City and Los Angeles, Canadian camps at Val Morin and Montreal, and a winter location on Paradise Island in the Bahamas. The selfless Swami, who came to me in faded robe and worn-out sandals, who drove a broken-down car from the west coast sans money, sans American driver's license, now flies his own private plane and expertly directs a work whose influence cannot be measured merely by saying he has some 200,000 followers.

According to all who know him, he is still a selfless

missionary of eastern philosophy with a remarkable capacity to handle with humility the greatness that has come to him. Though he is often satirized as "the flying Swamiji," he still has a disregard for worldly goods and an energy governed by the quiet calm of one who practices an inner timelessness. He still continues his discipline of pre-dawn meditation in what has been called the silence and innocence of the presence of God.

When any philosophical system achieves what the Christian philosophical system claims to achieve and doesn't, we may depend upon it that the system which effects the demonstration is the one that will attract the new generation of seekers. They have become that pragmatic as they shop around in the marketplace of faith.

I saw signs of this when Vishnudevananda was my guest. I know how his disciplines impressed me. I became aware of the power of the process when a following of yoga enthusiasts out of my university classes grew into what is now the Sivananda Yoga Order. I followed its progress as it expanded from a loosely knit campus workshop to a closely knit community of devotees around the world. The parenthetical time between the day Swami came to my home and the present is approximately fifteen years. And I am thinking to myself how quickly an idea takes hold when its time and its embodiment in a man have come.

2

Make no mistake about it, yoga is a powerful and persuasive stranger at our door. In its religious and integrative meaning it has many connotations. Derived from the Sanskrit *yuj,* equivalent to the English "yoke," it is defined as a method of uniting the personal self and the impersonal Self. It is a bond that effects a union with our highest consciousness. It represents a series of paths to Self-unfoldment and Self-realization, a bridge between spirit and matter, a philosophical system aiming at the attainment of *moksha* or salvation. It is all this, but most of all it is a discipline effectively unifying body, mind, and spirit into an instrument for more perfectly manifesting the presence of God. Vedanta explains it philosophically, yoga demonstrates it in practical techniques.

This is particularly true of Hatha Yoga, which lays great emphasis on physical postures (*asanas*), on effective breathing *(pranayama),* on right thoughts, right actions, right concentration, and right affirmations *(mantras).* The goal of Hatha Yoga is the integration of the total person within himself and his environment. It goes along with the current saying, "The environment that lives in you." Its target is the recognition that life is a trinity, interrelating the physical, mental, and spiritual components of man.

The word Hatha, composed of *ha* (sun) and *tha* (moon), symbolically suggests that the positive and negative energies of these two heavenly bodies should be harnessed and harmonized, as should all positive and negative energies, in order to realize an effective, balanced life. This is done largely by utilizing the positive and negative "vital air" *(prana)* through scientific breathing. The regulation of the vital air steadies the mind, and the mind in turn controls and regulates the *pranic* life force.

Hatha Yoga, the yoga usually thought of when one speaks of yoga in America, has developed its technique into an elaborate system built around an incredible series of postures, or *asanas*, of which there are literally thousands of variations. Some are simple positions easily assumed, others are so complex that only a highly skilled devotee can ever hope to accomplish them.

It helps immeasurably to bear the yoke of yoga in one's youth. The physical dexterity required is more related to the ballet than to calesthenics. Timing, grace, ease, and subtlety of execution are part of Hatha Yoga's secrets. The idea is to build harmony and rhythm rather than muscle and brawn. A yoga teacher said to me, "If you do not feel refreshed when you have done the *asanas*, you are not doing them properly."

As I have said, it helps if you are young. It also helps if you are an Indian or an Oriental accustomed to squat and sit crosslegged, and conditioned to look upon the body as a supple vehicle of life, naturally relaxed, capable of being controlled.

There are, of course, always exceptions in this matter of both youth and nationality. I know a European woman, currently a teacher in the Val Morin yoga camp, who in her early sixties was arthritic, stiff-jointed, and in such deteriorating condition she was given up to die. She embraced Hatha Yoga as a way of life, faithfully followed prescribed dietary regulations, disciplined her mind in yoga philosophy and her body in yoga "exercises," and today, some ten years later, she is a picture of health, demonstrating the most difficult *asanas* with apparent ease and skill.

I saw her beautifully executed shoulder stands *(sarvangasana),* headstands *(sirhasana),* lotus postures *(padmasana),* and even the intricate *matsyana,* or fish posture, which begins with the lotus position (right foot on left thigh and left over right on the right thigh, spine erect), and while seated in this position lowering the body backward until the *top* of head rests on the floor, hands grasping toes and breathing relaxed. They say it's an excellent therapy for the thyroid!

What has this to do with "religion"? Everything, if you remember that the postures properly executed always combine body, mind, and spirit in an awareness of Self as God's expression.

A chiropractor friend of mine named Clay Thompson, who knew nothing about yoga, got hold of a book on the subject, and put aside a special period every morning and night to practice the *asanas* and *pranayama.* Since he was in his early fifties, there was a good chance that he would benefit from all this, as people of all ages do, but there was little hope, I felt, that he would get very far. Some two months after he began his study I received a copy of a Sunday supplement in which an illustrated story reported the astounding demonstrations of "a new yoga adept, a *cheala* (yoga disciple) who enthralled a Rotary Club convention with postures usually requiring years of study and discipline." There was Dr. Thompson doing headstands, lotus postures, and going the whole course on an improvised platform looking for all the world like a swami. He could not quite convince me that he had been a yogi in a previous incarnation, but he did prove that the awareness of complete synchronization of body, mind, and spirit can work yogic wonders, improve the body, sharpen the intellect, deepen the consciousness, and give the initiate a thorough and total "conversion" experience.

For the point is totally missed if Hatha Yoga is construed merely as a course in physical fitness. It *is* a way of life, a faith, a discipline to such a degree that it is popularly considered a religion. Though you can certainly belong to *any* religion and engage in yoga practices. And this is exactly what the yoga strangers at our door are telling us. They are daring us to be stronger, live longer, and be better disciplined than most of us who have had the church as the training ground for the good life most of our days.

There is a great difference between merely practicing yoga and being a *yogi*. The European woman would, of course, be considered more of a yogi than my friend Dr. Thompson, because she has embraced not only the regimen but has dedicated her life to the total philosophical content of yoga. The true yogi makes the spiritual life his vocation. He is deeply involved in yoga's tradition, has been thoroughly trained by a master teacher, is dedicated to the rules and principles of selflessness, purity, celibacy, and the goal of God-realization.

Hatha Yoga's supportive philosophy teaches that the mind functions on three levels. First is the subconscious, instinctive, or automatic plane of being, controlling the involuntary functions of the body which can, in turn, be brought into submission through the use of the *asanas*. Second is the conscious mind, or intellect, controlling and guiding the subconscious and effecting the ego or "I" consciousness, ruled by the proper use of the vital force, *prana*. Third is the superconscious mind, capable of intuitive and beatific awareness, which is increased by the proper application of positive affirmations and vibrations of *mantras*.

Beyond these three levels is "pure consciousness," which is reached when one is in full mastery of body, mind, and spirit, and recognizes this total wholeness as divine Self, formless, timeless, infinite. The Self in this realm of reality is one with God. The *Tat Tvam Asi* (That Art Thou) of Hinduism is the highest aphorism on the yogic path.

The degree to which this unitive Self-with-God is manifested is a touchstone for the level of spiritual consciousness. A true yogi finds it difficult to believe, as many Christians also do, that objectively administered acts or preachments or sacraments can be effective without a deep subjective dedication. Yogis say:

Anything you preach without living the truth of it is hypocrisy and can have no effect for good.

You can get an estimate of a man's physical life by his mental and spiritual attitudes.

One who makes a conscious act of breathing may be depended upon to make a conscious act of thinking.

He who has no constructive control over his actions can have no constructive control over the actions of others.

There is no greater joy than the knowledge that Self wins over self, and no greater triumph than the victory of Self over matter.

Unless a man lives according to his convictions, he has no convictions.

The basis of the higher spiritual life is ethical life. Without ethical perfection, Self-realization is impossible.

The greatest defect in any religion, yogis contend, is the ease with which men allow a gap to exist between spiritual principles professed and moral acts practiced. This, they readily admit, is also the greatest defect in yoga. Who dares preach about the breath of life and then not demonstrate that his life is sustained by proper breathing? How can a man speak about the body as the temple of God and then willfully defile it? Close the gap between morality and moral conduct. Close the gap between professed faith in God and faith in action.

But if this has been made to sound harsh and dogmatic, the wrong impression has been conveyed. The true *joy* of life is in closing the gap, and there should never be any compulsion. "True yoga is fun!" is a favorite saying among young followers of yoga philosophy. Master teachers who have invaded our western world, from Yogananda to Vishnudevananda, have by no means interpreted yoga in terms of painful austerities, renunciation of the world, or self-negation. Yoga, to them, is life affirmation based on faith in God's laws, filled with the thrill of God-awareness, and demonstrated in physical, mental, and spiritual fitness of the kind God intended man to enjoy.

3

As I watched the extraordinary rise of interest in yoga and was an eye-witness to Hatha Yoga centers springing up across the country, as I saw books on the subject burgeon into best sellers and as libraries cited phenomenal interest in yoga texts, I often asked myself, "What is yoga's appeal?"

How account for the fact that people flock to a midweek yoga-training session, but refuse to attend a midweek church service? Why did my students respond to the prescribed disciplines set down by Vishnudevananda? Many of these young people, who wouldn't have attended a ten o'clock chapel service to save their souls, got up at five-thirty to meet in a cold classroom and engage in yoga postures, chant yoga *mantras,* practice controlled breathing, and sit together in silent meditation.

Why?

Is it India that creates the glamour and the fantasy? Hardly. Most American travelers are shocked at the suffering and starvation and lack of activism on the part of the Indian masses. There is little in the subcontinent to make an Occidental envious of the average Hindu's lot in life. Visit the so-called holy cities and you are struck by the sight of emaciated beggars, bedraggled pilgrims, and skin-and-bone holy men seated in the dust and ruin of decaying shrines. Drift down the sacred rivers and you are taken aback by the hawkers or morbidly entranced by the sight and scent of smoldering funeral fires.

Journey to Indian *ashrams,* and you instinctively contrast them with the churches and spiritual retreats in America. Chances are, you conclude, that in appearance and comfort at least, there was no reason for your ever leaving home, and if cleanliness is next to godliness, you might better have made your reservation at any church camp anywhere in the U.S.A.

What is yoga's appeal? The promise of healthier, longer life? Hardly. The mortality rate in India is 12.9

per 1000. Life expectancy is 47 years. America has a mortality rate of 9.7 and our life-span is roughly 69. We can talk about faith, fun, and fitness being basic in yoga teaching, but where do you find evidences of these expressions in Indian life?

What is yoga's appeal? Because the matter of longevity and health were so often stressed, I gave a thought to some of yoga's exponents and the years of their lives. It was true that they usually outlived the national average of their time. The renowned Sivananda made his transition at the age of 70. Sir Aurobindo was active until his death at 78. T. S. Vaswani was liberated at 78. Ramakrishna embraced *mahasamadhi* after reaching 50. His chief disciple, Vivekananda, entered final illumination at 39. Patanjali, most eminent of yogis who lived some three centuries before the time of Christ, is said by some to have died at 33, while others report he lived to be 60.

We could, of course, match this list with an impressive roster of non-yogis who outlasted their contemporaries much more spectacularly. Albert Schweitzer, who, safe to say, never stood on his head, was active and alert at 85. Winston Churchill, who practiced few, if any, yoga disciplines, drank a toast to his own health at 91. Harry Emerson Fosdick, who never did a shoulder stand, wrote to me when he was 85. I saw J. C. Penney celebrate his ninetieth birthday looking hale and hearty. Pope John, who probably never deigned to sit lotus fashion, made his ascension at 82. And I get to wondering how great an array of religious, political, and industrial figures are still going strong without the benefit of *asanas* or the blessings of *pranayama!* Of course, there is always the hypothetical suggestion that they would have been even more productive and lived even longer if they had embraced yogic teachings somewhere along the way!

What is yoga's appeal? Is it our love for the body beautiful, which youthful yogis portray so magnificently in their artistry? I once described Vishnudevananda's demonstrations as "music in motion." Is it the hidden dynamism which we sense in those who engage in yoga seriously? Are we perhaps conscious of the therapeutic value of Hatha Yoga, realizing that we could all use help in posture, breathing, and in a regimen for better living? Or is there a thrill in crossing cultural lines, and are we glamorized by Sanskrit phrases, quotations from Hindu holy books, and chants to the musical-sounding names of Hindu gods?

I thought for a time that western interest in yoga might have been prompted by two powerful forces in American life: a desire for inner tranquility and a wish for universal peace. But yoga, though it stresses the peace principle and intones vibrations to induce mental calm, is not necessarily more ambitious in these areas than the average Christian fellowship. Nor can yoga's appeal be justified only by its emphasis on meditation and prayer. All religions have distinctives in these fields.

The best answer can be found in a twofold need of which many of us are deeply conscious: first, our desperate search for synthesis and meaning in life, and second, our growing conviction that Christianity has told us only half the story about our relationship with God and Self.

Our need for synthesis. That our culture has left

us schizophrenic is a fact that strikes directly at religion and education. Accusations are widespread that churches preach doctrines which are no longer practiced, and that schools teach concepts no longer believed.

In our religions we are told to turn the other cheek, walk the second mile, love our enemies, and live out what the mod generation has called "all the other goodies of the gospel." But no one seems anxious or able to demonstrate their workability or prove their merit. In fact, there seems to be general agreement with the growing belief that if we followed Christ's injunctions literally in our kind of world, it *would* mean sudden death.

If many clerics and evangelists preach a gospel they do not fully live, many educators teach a morality they do not believe in, a social ethic they secretly question, and a cultural traditionalism they privately feel is an impediment to growth.

We are split personalities, divided in our sense of loyalties not only in religion and learning but in politics, business ethics, social action, in our attitude toward the communication media, in our reaction to agencies of health and healing, and most of all in our inability to live an integrated life and find substance in the reason for being.

In view of all this, yoga has a special appeal. It offers a challenge to an integrated life. It puts responsibility squarely on the individual and dares him to view himself as a total person: body, mind, and spirit.

Health and well-being, the enticing spell of the *asanas,* the thrill of *pranayama,* the transforming power of the *mantras,* these are steps toward the self-integrative process. The introduction to new attributes of God, the sound of new tones said to set cosmic forces into vibration, the sight of so-called holy men who bear within themselves a secret charisma, these factors are no longer representative of Hinduism as a religion or of India as a nation. Yoga presents them as universal and basic in the life of every sincere seeker who feels the need for harmonization within himself before he can ever hope to make his contribution toward stabilization in his environmental world.

Believing this, an initiate discovers that one yogic breath gets him off to a great start, because there is something he *feels,* and feeling *knows.* One simple posture and he is on the threshold of a new discovery. One earnest *mantra* properly intoned and affirmed in a moment of subjective release, and prayer has a new dimension. One involvement with a class in yoga and you have entered a fellowship keenly aware of a mystic kinship. Almost instantly you are swept by a flood of inner awareness waiting to be released. You sense it by a telegraphic cosmic signal in your body.

As to this mysterious power, yoga has given it a name: *kundalini sakti,* and even the words get hold of you. *Kundalini,* the serpent power, the symbolic, mythological symbol of life is, according to yoga, more than a symbol. It is psychic energy in escrow. It is an innate force, coiled at the base of the spine, ready to be released by yogic practice and allowed to flow through nerve centers into mind and spirit. What I am saying is that yoga promises its followers the recognition and experience of "Absolute Being" which, veiled by its own presence, finally reveals itself as "Self-in-God," and the initiate is no longer separated or alone in an otherwise separated and lonely world.

He has entered into the awareness of an integrated being, and this is the first half of yoga's modern appeal.

4

The second major reason for yoga's attractiveness to the western world can be traced to a growing belief that Christianity held back some basic teachings and let others go by default when Christ's teachings segued from a spontaneous fellowship of the spirit into a jurisdictionally structured corporate body. In this transition, many Christians believe the deeper, more exacting personal features of the Galilean's esoteric counsel were forfeited in favor of institutionalized forms and ecclesiastical rituals. Now they are asking whether the "Divine Light" shifted from demonstrations of the true Self to a necessary defense of the "true church."

There has, of course, always been a speculation that Jesus was influenced by yoga and that he influenced yoga in return. Where was he during his "hidden years" from twelve to thirty? Did he actually die at the age of thirty-three or could it have been, as Irenaeus, Bishop of Lyons insisted, that Jesus lived to a ripe old age? Was he a member of the Essenes? Was his story, like the Masonic account of Hiram Abiff, part of a secret initiatory ritual, the treasured property of both Christian and non-Christian fraternities? Was he an initiate of Greek and Asiatic esoteric groups? The reports have never quieted among those who try to give continuity to his life, that he studied in India and Greece, visited Tibet, and that a record exists in a Buddhist monastery in Ceylon proving that Jesus of Nazareth made a prolonged retreat among the brethren of the order. Small wonder that yoga enthusiasts deliberately lay claim to him and even go so far as to assume that when he said, "take my yoke upon you" he had the yoke of yoga clearly in mind.

Swami Vivekananda once had a dream. He dreamed that Jesus never lived, but that the Savior's name was an attempt to personify the truths taught by the Therapeutae, a group of ascetics living near Alexandria, Egypt. Vivekananda insisted that the Therapeutae took their name from *"Thera,"* a Buddhist monk, and added the suffix *"putra,"* Sanskrit for "son." Convincing as the dream was for this renowned swami, he nonetheless loved the story of Jesus, and said that if such a man had actually existed, "I would have washed his feet not with my tears only, but with my heart's blood."

Jesus is also referred to in yogic history by virtue of the fact that his practice of celibacy, his frequent retirement to the desert and the wilderness, his fasting, his tendency to teach through parables, and his miracles all fit the yogic pattern better even than the pattern of the Essenes. True yogis believe that all great religions begin with ethics. "Without truth, noninjury, continence, nonstealing, cleanliness, austerity, there can be no spirituality, and that is what their yogic master Jesus came to teach.

Apart from this there is an increasing belief that esoteric teachings and doctrines known to Christ and his disciples were jealously guarded by the church and were then lost by default, becoming the property of secret societies and lodges of various sorts and of yoga in particular. Yoga believes it is the custodian of much of this hidden wisdom, and it is ready to share it with those who have the will and the commitment to develop it in themselves. Jesus' ability to control the elements, walk on water, foresee, foretell, heal, and appear and disappear at will, are all part of the phenomena and demonstrations attributed to masters of the yogic art.

Hindus were often annoyed to hear Christian missionaries make claims about the miracles of Jesus as though Hinduism had no such claims in its repertory of faith. The fact is it *did* have them, and the story is told that Vivekananda once became so irritated with two evangelists who tried to convert him during an ocean voyage that he seized one by the throat and threatened to throw him overboard. The missionary, it is said, promised on his honor never to try to Christianize a yogi again.

Something tells us there *are* spiritual needs in our lives and spiritual voids in our thinking which the church should be able to fill with techniques and actual demonstrations. Something tells us we are unlimited. There is no vision of health which we should not rightly realize and enjoy if we really know the secrets of divine law. There is no limit to our reach of mind and outreach of spirit if we but had the proper understanding. There are no doors which could be closed to us if we had the proper key. The things Jesus did *should* be ours to perform and the promises he made should somehow be ours to live. There is no situation which should not yield to a spiritual law, bend to a spiritual power, or be solved by a spiritual force if someone would only pass on to us the enlightenment he had!

The *samadhi* of yoga, so much like the Christian state of mystic trance, tempts us to turn to the teaching of swamis. *Satwapatti,* the attainment of a state of purity, so perfectly demonstrated by Jesus, has not been duplicated for us better than by yogic masters. We feel there is a secret teaching we have missed. *Sukshma Sharira,* control of the astral body, is tempting in its implications, and we wonder where the Christ teaching in this field can again be found. We, too, should be able to still the waves of the sea, control the forces of nature, and draw forth and give out love and peace and health and life, if only we had the secret teaching, for didn't he himself say that greater things than his would be ours to do?

5

I not only let the stranger Yoga in when he came rapping at my door, I assured him he could stay, although some churchly friends of mine were sure such intimacy would profane my "orthodox convictions." I felt it would enrich them. And it did. All of this was even before my views were substantiated by the appearance of *Christian* Yoga (1960) in which the courageous Benedictine monk, Father Déchanet, went on record to say, "Every day the exercises, and indeed the whole ascetic discipline of yoga, make it easier for the grace of Christ to flow in me. I feel my hunger for God growing, and my thirst for righteousness, and my desire to be a Christian in the full strength of the word—to be for Christ, to be of Christ, without any half measures or reservations."

I assured Yoga it could stay. I needed it. True, my parental faith had always advocated the union and yoke of body, mind, and spirit. Pregnant in the gospel were implications that assignment to be a follower of Christ demanded "all that in me is." Somewhere in my deeper skirmishes with my church I had always been alerted to the discipline of meditation, the value and force of moral fortitude, the need for study which would show me approved of God, a workman unashamed, rightly dividing the Word of truth. Terms like "a quiet time for prayer," the "inner shrine of awareness," the need to "watch and pray and fast," the glory of "losing oneself in the consciousness of the cosmic," all had been brought to my attention, but somehow yoga brought them into life.

One of my basic beliefs has always been that every life eventually reveals a divine timing in its unfoldment, but that still does not assuage a feeling of self-reproach when I think how long I waited to let this stranger in. Fortunate the person who finds Hatha Yoga early in life and takes it seriously! Lucky for him who understands why it is occasionally helpful to stand on his head! Good for her who goes into yoga for any reason: health, beauty, religion, curiosity, sharpening of the wits or rubbing out of wrinkles, or finding a secret source of power to meet life on its own! Pity the person who prejudges without investigation, and too bad for him who sees this stranger as contradictory rather than as complementary to the overview of life!

All of this may do little more than popularize the outer aspect of Hatha Yoga. It may even give the mistaken impression that yoga is, at best, a form of physical and mental culture. While this may justify it, the fact remains that yoga's greatest merit lies in its technique for total purification of life. Actually its deepest principles beat at the heart of every great religion. Yoga is an empiric way toward proof of faith, proof, too, that there can be a positive and absolute union of the individual soul and the universal soul no matter how one's particular religion may construe these terms.

I used to marvel at the public interest in the life and teaching of Paramahansas Yogananda. His *Autobiography of a Yogi* has been an outstanding best seller for many years. His Self-Realization Fellowship Centers in various parts of the world are favorite retreats for sincerely seeking souls. He was, of course, a colorful figure. I remember the impression he made on me when I met him in his Mt. Washington mansion in greater Los Angeles in 1950. I was told by an awed devotee that his master had been in *samadhi* for three days. When Yogananda appeared on the great stairway he seemed still to be in a trancelike state. Eyes partially closed, luxuriant black hair hanging over his shoulders, voice suitably hushed, he was convincingly messianic. His loose-fitting, saffron-colored robe covered a strong body, and the dynamic of his presence charged the room with charismatic force. I remember my romantic thinking, "He carries the longing of the universe together with its joy." There was a sense of peace about him not quite of this world and a serenity beyond the kind we commonly look for in our daily quest.

The reason for his popularity was obvious. After all, this dramatic, successful exponent of eastern thought was a disciple of the renowned guru Mahavatar Babaji, and he had been instrumental in establishing picturesque headquarters in the Hollywood area in the days when Los Angeles was competitive, with showmanship-religion all the way from flamboyant Aimee Semple MacPherson who built Angelus Temple, to the millionaire religionist, James Fifield, who fought for "flag and freedom" out of his palatial Gothic Congregational Cathedral on Hoover Street. The west coast was alive and bristling with religious interest, and Yogananda was a sparkling figure in this fluid scene.

His success was more than glamour. He had a secret, the secret of Kriya Yoga (the yoga of universal action) which today is the main contender, along with Hatha Yoga, for the interest and attention of the western world. Yogananda succeeded in making Kriya Yoga work in changing lives and in giving direction to lives and in synthesizing lives into meaningful attitudes. This was the main reason for his influence. It is also the answer to the uninterrupted sales of his *Autobiography*.

"Kriya," says the text, "overcomes the tug-of-war between the mind- and the matter-entangled senses, and frees the devotee to reinherit his eternal kingdom. He knows then that his real being is bound neither by physical encasement nor by breath—symbol of mortal man's enslavement to air, to Nature's elemental compulsions. Master of his body and mind, the Kriya Yogi ultimately achieves victory over the last enemy, Death."

That "last enemy" summoned Yogananda himself

with startling suddenness, but it also instantly lifted him into greater prominence than ever before. His passing, according to his followers, proved beyond any possible doubt that he was indeed a divine incarnation and a guru supreme.

On March 6, 1952, Yogananda had serenely told a group of his disciples, "I have a big day tomorrow. Wish me luck." On the following day he went to the Biltmore Hotel to speak at a banquet honoring the new Indian ambassador. Yogananda ate sparingly of vegetables, as was his custom, nibbled at a strawberry parfait, then rose to deliver an eloquent address on Mother India and her spiritual heritage. His disciples still remember his words and never cease to thrill at his affectionate closing: "Where Ganges, woods, Himalayan caves, and men dream God; I am hallowed that my body touched that sod."

Pausing in the after-hush of these words, he raised his eyes and permitted his body to slump to the floor, dead.

This, we are told, is true *mahasamadhi,* a conscious, willing, gracious exit of the spirit from its physical home. Medical authorities attributed his death to "acute coronary occlusion" but that hardly explained the "prophecy" of "I have a big day tomorrow," or told his devotees anything about the mystery and wonder of their guru's power. Only they knew that. And even today medical science is still divided on the epilogue of this drama, for at Forest Lawn Cemetery where the body was embalmed, mortuary director Harry Rowe went on record to say, "No sign of physical disintegration was visible in Yogananda's body even twenty days after death. . . . This state of perfect preservation is, so far as we know from mortuary annals, an unparalleled one. . . . At the time of receiving the body, the mortuary personnel expected to observe the usual progressive signs of bodily decay. Our astonishment increased as day followed day without bringing any visible change. . . . Yogananda's body was apparently in a phenomenal state of immutability and no odor of decay emanted from his body at any time."

He was 59. Today his body lies enshrined in Forest Lawn's "Room of the Golden Slumber," and is the object of many pilgrimages.

All of which is interesting enough and a powerful testimony to the teachings of Kriya. But yoga, as we have said, is many paths. Out of the philosophy of Patanjali, who first gave yoga teachings literary form in his famous *Yogasutra,* have come many yogic methods. There is, for example, Karma Yoga, a way of achieving union with God through service, similar to the mystical element in Christianity's concept of salvation through works. There is Mantra Yoga, union with God through prayer; Bhakti Yoga, union through love; Jnana Yoga, union through right knowledge; Raja Yoga, the yoga of the spiritual will, and so on.

In short, there are many yogas and I am glad for that. For though we believe there is but one universal mind, surely we all have minds of our own, and though we affirm there is but one state of consciousness, we often seem startlingly different from others. Though there is undoubtedly but one universal nature, each of us can recognize within ourselves that nature individualized. Though we all look alike, we all look different, and though we may all be talented, we are certainly not all talented in the same fields.

Often when I do my "yoga thing" and in an extra-special moment of awareness feel myself close to the edge of something superconscious, when I feel for a fleeting instant my oneness with all spiritual masters and all people and sense their aspirations, there often comes an enveloping, consuming power of love which, time and time again, takes form, and always for me, the form of God in Christ.

Yogis tell me this is great but add, "Now go beyond it! Let yourself go beyond form into the formless! Sublimate that sentiment, transcend it, and you are free!"

This, it seems to me, is part of the challenge and a good deal of the glory in finding these intriguing strangers at our door.

4

Unity of All Nations

1

Wherever I have gone to research the faith called
Baha'i, I have been astonished at what I have found.
This was true in Haifa when I visited their World Center and stood on Mt. Carmel in the shadow of the
jewellike Shrine of the Bab. Like the Taj Mahal, this
golden-domed structure is both a significant work of
art and a sacred tomb. Within its granite walls rests
the body of the forerunner of the Baha'i faith, the Bab,
which means "the Gate," and also the remains of
Abdul-Baha. The latter was the Baha'i leader who, on
a May day in 1912, placed a fieldstone in a barren
meadow in Wilmette, Illinois, and said prophetically,
"The temple is already built!"

His words came true in the *Mashriqu'l-Adhkar*
(Temple of the Great Peace), a multi-million-dollar wonder of the religious world. It was paid for exclusively

by Baha'is, and represents a new style of architecture which annually impresses a million tourists with its quietude and majestic charm.

I was equally astonished at the Baha'i "Nine-Year Plan" projected for the period 1964-73. During these years 65 new National Spiritual Assemblies are being incorporated, 70 new world territories will be opened, translations of Baha'i literature will reach 133 languages, 32 new teaching institutes will be established, 95 countries will recognize Baha'i holy days, there will be a widening and a strengthening of the relationship between the Baha'i community and the United Nations, two new temples will be built, bringing the total number to six: Wilmette, Frankfurt, Sydney, Kampala, Panama City, and Teheran.

But most of all, I am continually intrigued by the Baha'i people, close to a million of them representing the basic cultural and ethnic groups around the world and embracing obscure and little-known localities in far-flung lands where even Christianity has barely gone. Each Baha'i is a vocational missionary, and each forms a closely knit link in a circle of faith around the world.

They serve for free. They are professional teachers, industrialists, doctors, travel agents, farmers, and housewives, all dedicated to the propagation of the Baha'i Cause. I have met them in the most unexpected places, in a war-torn village in southeast Asia, in African cities, in industrial Mexico, in the executive branches of big industry in Iran, in schools and colleges on foreign campuses, in American cities and villages, wherever people dream of the age-old concept of the brotherhood of man and the fatherhood of God, somewhere in the unfolding rapture of the phrase, the Baha'is are there.

They are in Vietnam and in the Middle East, not to do battle, but to do good. They have put down their roots in Russia and have advocated understanding among the dissident masses of India. I will never forget the young American Baha'i couple, schoolteachers, in the war-ravaged, dung-filled streets of Pusan, Korea. The coed-appearing mother held her firstborn in her arms and told me with a matter-of-fact calm that she was sure God was working out his will and way in her life and in the world.

Part of the reason for my astonishment is the selfless commitment and the apparent lack of gimmicks involved in this relatively new and expanding faith. In a day when church growth is still graphically measured by accessions to denominational membership and the success of financial campaigns, the Baha'is stress the idea of a "Parliament of Religions," international workshops, interreligious relations, and refuse to accept money from anyone but a Baha'i. Here is strictly a layman's religion, without the benefit of clergy and a minimum of theological emphasis.

A significantly intellectual, world-conscious people, the Baha'is give the impression of being guileless to a fault. They seem to believe with heart and soul that world peace is a major issue and that they have been entrusted with God's plan for the unity of all nations. This in the very teeth of a world constantly at war and consistently bent on raising hell.

The Baha'i will not be deterred. He has a Messiah whose teachings he has embraced against the patronizing, pitying smiles of a skeptic world. This leader is Baha'u'llah, and among his beatitudes is, "Blessed are they who shall proclaim the doctrine of spiritual brotherhood, for they shall be called the Children of Light!"

That is the literal meaning of Baha'i, a "Child of Light," but "child of Baha'u'llah" would do just as well. He was the "Promised One" whom the Bab had proclaimed. Born Mirza Husayn Ali in 1817, son of a wealthy Persian nobleman, he joined the "Babis" early in life, abandoning fame, fortune, and royal friends to follow a vision which had commanded him to bring discordant religions and nations to a recognition of the divinely inspired truth that, "The earth is one country and mankind its citizens." For this, it is claimed, he suffered persecution, ridicule, imprisonment, and death, but not before he had etched his utopian idealism on the minds of rulers and subjects of the major kingdoms of the world. His letters to these leaders comprise part of the *Sacred Scriptures of Baha'u'llah.*

The Baha'is have pledged themselves to get these same messages to the modern world by way of example, self-sacrifice, missionary effort, and through the United Nations. Of all the strangers at our doors, none are more committed to the spiritual implications of peace and goodwill than those who claim that this Persian prophet is on a spiritual par with Jesus, both in historical importance and in the divine manifestation as a Savior of all mankind.

2

The genesis of the Baha'i gospel goes back to 1844. Its prologue foreshadows all the elements of a universal religious drama: sacred writings, revelation, prophecy, idealism, martyrdom, and miracles. It was the latter that intrigued me when I first heard of the Baha'is and learned that long ago their leader, the Bab (the Gate) had been sentenced to death for instigating a reform movement in Iran. The story had it that he had been suspended by ropes from a crossbar in the city of Tabriz and hung there while the firing squad took aim. When the smoke of some two hundred rifles cleared, the Bab stood on the ground unhurt. The guns of his would-be executioners had miraculously severed the ropes and set him free.

The account, whether legendary or for real, was enough to stir my interest. The story lodged in my mind, heightened by the fact that the Bab had vowed he would not die until his mission to mankind had been fulfilled. The mission? The promise of the coming of a Messiah, a new Prophet who would save the universal soul of mankind as Jesus had sought to save the souls of individuals. Having made this clear, having rallied his followers with the expectation of this advent, the Bab submitted himself to the authorities, so that they could accomplish what they had failed to do before, snuff out his defenseless life under a blistering hail of gunfire.

So he died. And such was the prologue. The time was now 1850. The theme: the unity of all nations, all religions, all people. The accusation: that the fanatical followers of the Bab were anarchists. The opposition: organized religions and the state. The quality of the Babis: young intellectuals, college students, accused of drawing the innocent into their utopian plot.

In 1863 the curtain rose on the main event. In a garden in a suburb of Bagdhad called Rizwan, a group of Babis discussed their fate, their strategy, and their faith. Out of their ranks stepped one of their most talented and committed members, Mirza Husayn Ali. With charismatic fervor he proclaimed himself as he whom the Bab had foretold, namely Baha'u'llah, and in that moment he was recognized as such in the eyes of his beholders. In that instant, it was believed, prophecy was fulfilled, and on that night in Rizwan, the Babis became Baha'is and a new religion was born. On that night, too, a flood of persecution began which was to continue until Baha'u'llah died in 1892, a prisoner of the Turkish government at Acca in Palestine.

Modern Baha'is will never be daunted by persecution should it ever happen to them. They have the example of Baha'u'llah, the Splendor of God. His first exile was to Baghdad, even before his proclamation. His second and third were to Constantinople and to Adrianople in 1863. The fourth to Acca in 1868. Here he was incarcerated in the great fortress and spent his last years in a country house just north of the ancient city, at a place called Bahji, Israel.

I remember how moved I was when I visited that prison fortress where Baha'u'llah spent some twenty-five years. I remember my deep impressions when I went with a Baha'i to Bahji where the body of the "Promised One" lies reverently enshrined. Here, truly, was a man who promoted the first real rallying call for world peace. His words to sultans, kings, queens and popes are known to every Baha'i, "God has ordained as the sovereign remedy for the healing of the world, the union of all its people in one universal Cause, one common Faith." There was also another saying of Baha'u'llah which my Baha'i guide impressed upon me, "Let not a man glory in this, that he loves his country, let him rather glory in this, that he loves his kind."

Whenever I think of these words in view of war and violence and national unrest, I wonder whether this is why the Baha'i faith is growing and whether its religious universalism is also a reason for its being feared. After all, what will these strangers at our door do to man's delight in war-power, to our dedication to denominationalism, to our patriotism, and to our national pride? Or is it possible that one may love both one's country *and* one's kind?

3

The reason I am astonished at the growth of the Baha'i faith—in the past six years nearly six thousand new Spiritual Assemblies have been added—is because I brought the first Baha'i representative to my classroom at the University of Iowa almost twenty years ago. In those days Baha'u'llah was a strange-sounding name, and to many a fundamentalist Christian it was also a dirty word. A Baha'i was something of an oddity. The claim that Baha'u'llah was equal to Jesus was then, as now, intriguing to some and blasphemous to others. That he should speak as the mouthpiece of God was to many the height of heresy.

This was the period after World War II when, in the light of world unity, the League of Nations closed its doors (1946) and gave its physical assets to the United Nations. It was claimed by Baha'is that the writings of

Baha'u'llah had inspired the League and would have their influence on the U.N. This was the time when, in the light of tolerance and spiritual understanding, we were shocked by the assassination (1948) of Mahatma Gandhi. When in the light of world history the Free State of Israel (1948) had been proclaimed in Tel Aviv. And when, in the light of another brushfire war, the "Korean incident" was in the making. This was when I first began to recognize the stubborn challenge of Baha'u'llah's message as it was articulated by the Children of Light.

It was at about this time that I had written a book entitled *Report to Protestants* in which I recounted my futile efforts as a young minister trying to merge two churches, an Evangelical and a Baptist, which were separated by sixty feet of graveled road in a small Kansas town. While I was frustrated by my inability to bring these two hometown denominations together, here were Baha'is ambitiously planning to merge into spiritual unity not only churches but nations separated by thousands of years of religious, racial, and political dissension. Clearly such an assignment was too audacious to be disregarded, and too impressive not to be acclaimed by those who believed its message could be lived.

There was a young man in one of my classes, an Episcopalian, who was in love with a local Lutheran girl. Upon their engagement they encountered strong parental opposition from both sides, and were warned that unless they were married in the faith of their fathers there could obviously not be a wedding. It created quite a stir and both town and campus heard about it, but the couple said in effect, "A plague on both your houses" and became Baha'is.

That such an action would cause little more than a ripple these days clearly shows the course of the ecumenical stream. We have come even farther in our recognition that religions and cultures are no longer confined to stated boundaries or locked in racial or cultural lines. The churches I tried to get together not only united, but the issues that once divided them— historic, doctrinal, social—no longer pertain. I saw my parental denomination, the German Reformed, merge with the Evangelical Synod, then with the Congregational Church, which had already merged with the Christian Church (American Christian Convention), to form the United Church of Christ.

All of this happened in the span of some thirty years, and it is interesting to conjecture what could happen before the dawn of the twenty-first century if this trend continues, what spiritual conglomerates will arise, what syntheses will take place, what now-inconceivable unions will be effected, and where the faith called Baha'i will figure in the accelerating trend toward good fellows getting together in the name of justice, tolerance, and the brotherhood of man.

Catholics drop in rather regularly at Protestant services. Protestants are interested in Roman Catholicism's transition. Jews offer courses in Catholic seminaries. Catholics are guest professors in Protestant schools. Philosophy east and philosophy west are joining hands. Buddhist and Christian fight side by side and/or against each other on the world's battlefields. So do Moslems and Jews. Buddhism, Shinto, and Christianity are becoming ever more closely wedded. The Vatican distributes gifts to North and South Vietnam. Christian America sells military gear to both sides engaged in conflict in the Middle East.

The strangers at our door who call themselves the Children of Light are bearing the sacred scriptures of a new prophet in their hands. They are proclaiming his words from ninety-four National Spiritual Assemblies strategically situated around the globe. By means of public lectures, campus appearances and personal testimony, they are seeking to persuade us to get the message Baha'u'llah says:

> The world's equilibrium will be established through the vibrating influence of this most great, this new World Order! Mankind's ordered life will be revolutionized through the agency of this unique, this wondrous System, the like of which mortal eyes never witnessed. . . . With faces beaming with joy, hasten ye unto Him. This is the changeless Faith of God, eternal in the past, eternal in the future. Let him that seeketh, attain it; and as to him that refuses to seek it, verily, God is Self-Sufficient, above any need of His creatures.

4

Before Baha'u'llah died at the age of seventy-five, he appointed his eldest son, Abdul-Baha, as his successor. Also known as Abbas Effendi, he and his mother had shared exile and imprisonment with the prophet, and Abdul-Baha had grown to be more and more like his father in appearance, in thought, and in a sense of the sacredness of his mission. He was 49 at the time of Baha'u'llah's "ascension" in 1892 and was forced to remain a religious prisoner of the Turks until 1908, when a new regime overthrew the Ottoman Empire and set free all political and religious prisoners.

He set out on a number of journeys for the propagation of the Baha'i faith, visiting Egypt, Europe, and America, laying the foundations of the administrative order of his father's work, an order already enshrined in Baha'u'llah's revelation. In 1920 he accepted a knighthood of the British Empire from George V and, as has been said, he broke ground in Wilmette, Illinois, for the North American "House of Justice."

"The religion of the Baha'is," said the *Boston Congregationalist* during the American visit of Abdul-Baha, "has nothing of the eccentricity of faddism of so many modern religions and none of their shallow philosophy. It is simply a synthesis of the noblest ethics of the world around one common center, love and goodwill to all men."

"Abdul-Baha," said the president of Leland Stanford University, "will surely unite East and West, for he treads the mystical way with practical feet."

But that is past history. Today Baha'is are pressing America and the world to take a hard look at the practicality of the tenets of their faith. I see them becoming ever more courageous, sure of themselves, confident of the divinity of Baha'u'llah, committed to the conviction that they are ordained as leaders in the apocalyptic crisis of our time. They insist their world religion is not eclectic, syncretic, or an offshoot of Judaism, Islam, Christianity, or any other movement or sect, nor does it derive its inspiration from the sacred books of other faiths. It is an independent world religion and its message, they insist, is a revelation direct from God through

Baha'u'llah, who made clear, however, that he, the human vehicle of this immortal truth, is never to be identified with "the Essence of Divinity itself."

One of the most significant steps toward the implementation of this "Essence of Divinity," however, was taken at the 1967 Intercontinental Conference of Baha'is held at the National Baha'i Center in Wilmette. Here the Baha'i Communities of North America issued their remarkable document, "Human Rights are God-given Rights," a statement which gave rise to NABOHR (North American Baha'i Office for Human Rights), and which pledged itself to "the elimination of all forms of racial discrimination, as a reaffirmation of the principle that all human beings are equal in dignity and rights."

It plans to work actively with the United Nations Conventions on genocide, on the elimination of discrimination, slavery, forced labor, on its plans for equality in employment, occupation, education, and religious convictions. It has set in motion plans for the dissemination of information to combat misconceptions and superstitions about race, the sponsoring of special conferences and workshops in the field of human rights, and the awarding of citations for achievements in these fields, recognition to be made on a "Human Rights Day" suggested as the tenth of December.

The recommendations for action included: that the Federal Government and states recognize American Indian treaty rights as agreed on and understood by Indians; that bilingual school systems with bilingual curriculum, teachers, and counselors be established for Mexican-Americans; that public schools be encouraged to hire more teachers from minority groups; that low-interest, governmental loans be made available to residents of the Spanish-American communities so that they can cooperatively purchase slum dwellings owned by absentee landlords and improve and rehabilitate these buildings; that all miscegenation laws be abolished; that race as a criteria for adoption of children be eliminated from the policies and procedures of adoption agencies; that the Federal Government be urged to ratify the remaining Human Rights Conventions and Covenants as set forth by the United Nations; and so on into the problems and challenges of social equality, to a degree unmatched by any other religious body, even the Unitarian-Universalists.

5

A friend of mine, an Episcopalian who read the printed report of the Baha'i resolutions mentioned above (available from NABOHR, 112 Linden Avenue, Wilmette, Illinois) remarked to me enigmatically that he felt the resolutions of the Episcopal Council which met at Charleston, S.C. in May, 1970, were more courageous. They called for total withdrawal of U.S. forces in Southeast Asia, support for student strikes against oppressive and unjust actions by the government, such as harassment of the Black Panther members, the killing of students on campuses by the National Guard and police forces, approval of the Cooper-Church restriction on military spending, and so on.

"And," he added significantly, "we are not asking anyone to accept a new prophet when we still haven't caught up with the teachings of the Christ."

This, perhaps, more than any other criticism of the Baha'i faith, is most widespread among members of the Christian community. "Why proclaim a new Messiah when the real Messiah still wanders homeless across the earth?"

The Baha'is have an incisive answer: the reason Jesus wanders homeless is because the world has not yet known or accepted the divinity of Baha'u'llah, who is Christ returned. His appearance was Christ's Second Coming. His advent was the fulfillment of prophecy. His pronouncements, according to Baha'i eschatologists, were those of Christ speaking once more to a wayward world.

"In all the revealed world religions," says George Townshend in his book *Christ and Baha'u'llah,* "the coming of the Kingdom is identified with the appearance of the Supreme World Redeemer, the Lord of Hosts, the returned Christ, the Qa'im, the new Buddha. One fold and one shepherd is to replace the many conflicting and separated groups of men. This outstanding pledge, originally given thousands of years ago, has never been taken up by any of the Great Prophets until the nineteenth century, when Baha'u'llah announced to the rulers and religious leaders of the world that He was this Redeemer and the Bearer of God's message to modern man. He proclaimed that He spoke with the Voice of God Himself, that He was the Lord of Hosts, Christ, come in the glory of the Father, and that his was indeed the Last Day, the Day of Judgment."

This brings us into the theological implications of this indomitable world religion. While most Christians believe that Jesus Christ was expressly sent by God to redeem mankind, most Baha'is are of the opinion that Baha'u'llah was divinely ordained by God to redeem Christianity. Again, the Word was made flesh. Just as in Christianity, the most persuasive testimony about his Messiahship came from Jesus himself, so among Baha'is: the cardinal credential about Baha'u'llah as a divine manifestation came directly from Mirza Husayn Ali. Throughout his writings and conversations he consistently made references to this identification.

This must be understood in order to properly understand the Baha'is. As in orthodox Christianity, salvation is attained through acceptance of Jesus as Savior, reconciling man to God, so in this modern movement issuing out of Haifa and Wilmette, *mankind* is reconciled to God through the atonement and mission of this Persian seer. Obviously, this places a much deeper perspective and implication on the Baha'i movement than a mere socially activistic program for world union. A direct relationship with God is here involved, and an understanding of the true "Church of God" is presented as a challenge to modern man.

In my earliest research among the Baha'is I met a woman who identified herself as a "Baha'i-Methodist." She held a copy of Baha'u'llah's *Hidden Words,* and she radiated Baha'i light.

"You know," she said, "none of the Baha'is have ever asked me to give up my church affiliation. To me this demonstrated what we really mean by the unity of all faiths. I'm a good Methodist and a good Baha'i. The Baha'i faith is a spirit. I think it is the only spirit that has the answer for all problems. I talk about it wherever I can, even to my missionary society. It is surprisingly easy to merge Methodism into the larger unity of Baha'i beliefs."

To this I would answer, "Not quite." While the concept of unity-in-diversity is a popular phrase in the Baha'i work and while it is a desideratum to gain moral and ethical support for the Cause from various church affiliates, you are really not a Baha'i until you are a full-fledged voting Baha'i, believing and living the principles of the faith, accepting Baha'u'llah as the Promised One and actively affiliating with a Baha'i Spiritual Assembly.

Baha'u'llah decreed that in every locality where nine or more adult believers reside, a Local Spiritual Assembly (House of Justice) should be formed. In countries or regions in which National Spiritual Assemblies (Secondary Houses of Justice) are provided for, the believers elect delegates to a national convention for the election of the National Assembly. Members of National Assemblies are the electors of the members of the Universal House of Justice. In addition to being the head of the faith and its supreme administrative Body, the Universal House of Justice has power to legislate on any matter not covered by the holy writings. The permanent seat of the Universal House of Justice is in Haifa, Israel.

To become a voting member of a Baha'i community, that is, to actually become a Baha'i, one must receive the approval of the Spiritual Assembly and prove that he possesses the qualifications for Baha'i faith and practice. This is not to say that our Baha'i-Methodist was not a good Baha'i in spirit and in truth, but there was still basically a matter of divided loyalties. Many people who retain membership in other denominations attend Baha'i meetings, support Baha'i activities and are closely identified with the movement, but, to repeat, a true Baha'i is a Baha'i community member.

He has his own sacred scriptures, foremost among them Baha'u'llah's mystical work, *Seven Valleys,* and his own book of wisdom, *Hidden Words;* he has his own laws, his own administrative institutions, his own holy places, the most sacred of which are situated on and near Mount Carmel. His religious beliefs are highly symbolic and metaphysical, couched in the idyllic mysticism of the east and adorned with the poetic charm of the apocalyptists.

If thou seekest to be intoxicated with the cup of the Most Mighty Gift, cut thyself from the world and be quit of self and desire.

The marriage of the Baha'is means that both man and woman must become spiritually and physically united, so that they may have eternal unity throughout all the divine worlds and improve the spiritual life of each other. This is Baha'i matrimony.

Know ye that the world is like unto a mirage which the thirsty one thinks to be water; its water is a vapor; its mercy a difficulty; its repose hardship and ordeal; leave it to its people and turn ye unto the Kingdom of your Lord the Merciful.

The Supper of the Lord which His Highness the Spirit ate with the apostles was a heavenly supper and not one of material bread and water, for material objects have no connection with spiritual objects.

Believing in reincarnation is one of the old tenets held by most nations and creeds . . . but all these sayings and superstitions are vanity in the sight of God.

The Baha'i believes in prayer, in spiritual healing, in the immortality of the soul and the necessity to live in obedience to the laws of God as interpreted by Baha'u'llah. But over and above all of this, he is known to the world as a worker and spokesman in the embodiment of mankind's unity in a world order where there is an abolition of racial, religious, national, class and color prejudice, realization of equality of the sexes, the use of an international auxiliary language, an unfettered search after truth, and the essential harmony of science and religion.

These are felt to be the basis of their appeal and the tenets with which they are enlisting the loyalties of people in search for meaning and truth.

6

There is, however, one factor greater than all of the above which I consider the most powerful and relevant to these particular strangers at our door. It is the reality of a world fraternity already created in microcosm by those who are full-fledged Baha'is without any hyphenated loyalties. I mean by this that a Baha'i can travel around the world and never be alone or lonely. He trusts his fellow Baha'is implicitly and they trust him. There is a common bond of faith that unites them, and this is remarkable in view of the fact that the membership represents a wide range of nationalities obedient to their homeland, a broad spectrum of color and culture, and an even wider spread in economic position. But whether rich or poor, colored or white, wise or otherwise, Baha'is are at home with Baha'is, and in our kind of world this is a precious heritage.

I was once privileged to meet Shoghi Effendi, successor to Abdul-Baha. He was, in fact, Abdul-Baha's eldest grandson and was a student at Balliol College, Oxford, when his grandfather died in 1921. He returned to Haifa to become "Guardian of the Faith," endowed with supreme authority to delineate the structure of the administrative order and to develop the Universal House of Justice. His guardianship lasted for thirty-six years, a period of great expansion of the faith throughout the world, and toward the end of his life I visited him in his home near the golden-domed Shrine of the Bab.

The room in which I met him was spacious and sparsely furnished. On a wall was a framed page from the writings of Abdul-Baha, which aside from an Oriental wall hanging was actually the only decoration. The large divan, chairs, and table were set in orderly fashion on the heavily carpeted floor, and there was a feeling of austerity about it all. It was a room of haunting sensations, I thought, rich with the fragrance of incense, an aura of something mysterious, a lingering atmosphere of peace contrasting sharply with the unrest and fear that everywhere seemed to brood over Palestine.

The Guardian entered with authority. He was a diminutive, dark-complexioned man dressed in western attire but wearing a fez. His clean-shaven face and slender figure registered indomitable strength. He walked with head up as if an entourage of the faithful might be following him. He welcomed me wtih a sensitivity that seemed to feel, rather than hear my words. I envied him the sense of security and holy mission in life that filled his fifty-seven years with confidence beyond doubt and above question.

"Is the Baha'i faith making an impact upon the world?" I asked.

"Religious revolution, social evolution stand at the door of our age," he proclaimed. "The dynasties of institutionalized religion and centralized political power are confounded by the Light of the Cause. A new world civilization is being born, a new day is dawning."

"Is the world more religious than it has been? Is it more spiritually inclined?"

"Man has let go of God, but God will not let go of man. Religions must face each other honestly. Let them recognize the faith and the prophet that can unite them. Men have been so absorbed in the study of theology they have neglected the study of life."

When I reminded him that there were many new religions which had made tremendous strides, even greater than the growth of the Baha'i Cause, he replied,

"The trouble with these new religions is that they are always offering the people something. People too often join a new religion, or even an old one, because they expect to get something out of it. Baha'is believe they have something to give."

And among the giving is the example of "brotherhood in action," a quality of trust and interrelationship that many religions and fraternal organizations have held as an ideal but have sought for in vain. Most Baha'is know other Baha'is personally. They are welcome in each others' homes. They enjoy philosophical discussions about the writings of Baha'u'llah, Abdul-Baha, and Shoghi Effendi. They have memorized a great many of the sacred writings. They love to quote the Guardian's words, "The fundamental principle (of Baha'is) is that religious truth is not absolute but relative, that divine revelation is a continuous and progressive process, that all great religions of the world are divine in origin, that their basic concepts are in harmony, their aims and purposes the same, that their teachings are facets of one truth, that they differ only in the nonessential aspects of their doctrines, and their missions represent successive stages in the spiritual evolution of human society."

Wherever I traveled, following my meeting with Shoghi Effendi, Baha'is, knowing of my visit, would say, "Let me shake the hand that shook the hand of the Guardian." So great was their admiration for him, so deep was their respect.

He did not appoint anyone to succeed him. Instead he instituted what is known as the "Hands of the Faith," nine qualified administrators and counselors with special functions, primarily the protection and teaching of the cardinal principles: oneness of mankind, oneness of God, oneness of religion, the inviolable trinity of Baha'i belief.

It was Shoghi Effendi who, even more than Baha'u'llah or Abdul-Baha, provided the strangers at our door with their passports to the kingdoms of the world. Prejudices, he avowed, do not exist among Baha'is and their affection for one another is a foreshadowing of the fraternalism that will some day exist throughout a Baha'i-oriented society.

Baha'is believe him. They intend to make his words come true, especially when he said, "This universal, this transcending love which the followers of the Baha'i Faith feel for their fellowmen, of whatever race, creed, class, or nation, is neither mysterious nor can it be said to have been artificially stimulated. It is both spontaneous and genuine. They whose hearts are warmed by the energizing influence of God's creative love cherish his creatures for his sake, and recognize in every human face a sign of his reflected glory. Of such men and women it may be truly said that to them every foreign land is a fatherland, and every fatherland a foreign land."

The rhetoric made his words memorable, and the content, Baha'is will tell you, has already been proved true.

5

Peace, Joy and Prosperity

1

Several years ago it was my assignment to escort eleven Japanese religious leaders across the United States' mainland. The idea was to show these representatives of Nippon's emerging religions how America lives and worships, and to initiate what was a "Pilot Party" in interreligious cooperation. These men represented some twenty million members of the highly progressive movements which have recently risen out of Buddhism and old Shinto. The faiths included were Rissho Koseikai, Konkokyo, the Itto-En, Soto Buddhism, Omoto, Jodo Shinshu, and Shinto representatives. Our interpreter was a Japanese Methodist layman, Colbert Kurokawa, executive secretary of the International Interfaith Fellowship of Kyoto and an eminently qualified scholar of the Japanese religious scene.

For thirty days we visited various religious head-

quarters, appeared on college campuses, met with con-
gregations important in our Judeo-Christian heritage,
familiarized ourselves with the work of metaphysical
groups, no less than with the programs of Islam, the
Baha'is, and even with such obscure fellowships as the
Amish and Hutterite people.

It was a significant and exciting tour, but nowhere
in the length and breadth of our country did I find anything to compare with the fervor and phenomenal
growth of the religions represented by my guests, the
"made in Japan" religions with which they were affili-
ated, either as leaders or spokesmen.

I had been to Japan several times, had made a movie
documentary, "Japan, Land of the Kami," and planned
to return. All of these experiences convinced me that
throughout these emerging religions of the Land of the
Rising Sun, the pattern is the same: unquestioned dedication to the leaders and the cause, unlimited cooperation in the plans for expansion, unselfish giving for the
propagation of the faith, unquestioned and uncritical
trust in the teachings.

To better understand the psychology involved in
such devotion and to grasp the full impact of PEACE,
JOY AND PROSPERITY, it is necessary to take a backward glance to the time, a short quarter-century ago,
when a new God was born because an old god died.

Emperor Hirohito was a god, and not particularly
self-styled either. The doctrine of his divinity went
back to the legendary creation of Japan, fixed in Japanese minds with the popular myth of the god and
goddess, Isanagi and Izanami, who had stood on a
floating bridge of heaven before the earth was formed.

With his jeweled spear, Isanagi stirred the amorphous void into an island paradise.

Isanagi and Izanami were *Kami,* beings both mortal and divine. We can best understand *Kami* in terms of spirit. What to us is the animating life principle or power within personal consciousness provides an insight into the Japanese view of *Kami.* There is less differentiation between *Kami* and man in Japanese thought than there is between spirit and man in the mind of the average Christian. To the Japanese, God as *Kami* is human enough to be fully comprehended.

There was no Christ figure in the evolution of Japanese religion. There are no "holy scriptures" as authoritative as the Bible is to us, no plan of salvation, no dogmas or creeds. In fact, there was not even a name for the religion of Japan until Buddhism was imported from Korea in the sixth century.

It was then that the word "Shinto" was coined to describe what had always been the subconscious belief of those who considered their world the cradle of creation. Formed of two Chinese ideograms, Shinto literally means the "way of the gods" *(Kami-no-Michi).* *Kami* was reaffirmed as the self-creative power expressed in and encompassing all that ever was or is.

Though Buddhism had come to stay and though Christianity hopefully invaded the islands in 1547 with cross and crucifix borne by the Jesuit Francis Xavier, neither religion ever lured the free and highly imaginative Nipponese from the object of his worship: the Kami concept and belief in the great Kami, Amaterasu Omikami, goddess of the sun. Nor did any foreign ideology shake Japan's belief in the legend of Isanagi and Izanami, whose bridge of heaven, symbolized by the torii, still stands before the entrance to every Shinto shrine.

Always there was the emperor, reigning supreme with the sun goddess enshrined in a golden mirror above his throne. Always there was Shinto, with its 100,000 shrines and priests, and its myriads of Kami, the gods of the way. But as time went on there were also underground religions becoming ever more formidable, many of them reactions against state-controlled Shinto, all the result of visions, revelations, miracles, and reinterpretations of the will of God. During World War II, the Emperor and the military considered these groups sufficiently threatening to their security to round up and imprison many of the leaders and followers on charges of *lese majesty*.

Then came the *Gotterdammerung*. The bombs that annihilated two cities struck terror into the heart of every Japanese. They shocked many of us Americans, too, who in our innocence had never believed that our country would justify such wholesale slaughter, even in the guise of the strategy of war. Certainly when the fireball burst over Hiroshima and Nagasaki, many an ancient deity was shaken from his throne.

On August 15, 1945, Hirohito, reduced to mortal stature, took to the radio to inform his people that Japan was prepared to surrender. The masses listened, many finding it impossible to adjust to the incredible "de-deification" of their god. A national plea was voiced that he at least be permitted to maintain his secular rule.

The Allies agreed. Conditionally they allowed Hirohito to retain his crown, but not his halo of divinity. In place of state Shinto and a sovereign who had ruled overly long as god, complete freedom of religion was granted to the subjects of the Kami way.

So the floodgates opened. The new religions, liberated by an offshore power, suddenly appeared in amazing strength and in uncounted numbers. They came in force, like liberating armies of the mind, prepared to capture the hearts and loyalties of those whom the *Kami* had seemingly forsaken. Rather, they were the *Kami* returned, the true *Kami*, the gods of the way whom the militarists had flaunted and denied. They came out of hiding and they came to stay, proving not only how powerful they had been among the common people even before the old god died, but already hinting of the day when their missionaries would be standing at the doors of those who once had vanquished them.

This, then, is the story of some of those emerging groups who rose from the underground and by way of an ingenious spiritual alchemy, transmuted defeat, despair, and destruction into PEACE, JOY AND PROSPERITY. Within their ranks we find the solid signs that their appeal has now extended to the western world, again causing us to wonder and to ask who and what was conquered, and by whom, when viewed in the light of faith.

2

The current impact of Japanese religions was impressed upon me when I met a young American in love with a new-found faith. Granted he was a hippie-type. He was also a birthright Christian, a Protestant, and he had given up his parental religion. He had been in Japan spending time with a spiritual group called Itto-En, the Garden of Light. Here in this interfaith community, just a step away from Yamashina near Kyoto, he found what he considered to be the Christ-way personified in a group of some three hundred people; average, ordinary people from various walks of life who had once been as disturbed by the world as he. Now they had all things in common, shunned riches, respected all religions, loved all men, lived in gratitude, worked selflessly for others, and radiated peace and joy.

What impressed him even more was that visitors continually dropped in at Itto-En to learn about this way of life. Often they remained for serious training. Those who went back to their vocations found their outlook on life singularly changed. Through the past fifty years a million and more people in Japan had been influenced by the gospel of Itto-En. So he made a decision. He was determined to start a Garden of Light in America, convinced that many young people in their twenties, his age, would welcome such a world-within-a-world where religion could be proved to work.

When I told him I had known the founder of Itto-En, the late Tenko Nishida, he was overawed. He claimed that the charisma of this Japanese saint was still alive in the life lived by the people he had come to love in the Garden of Light.

"Tenko-san was really a great soul, wasn't he?" he asked, and his voice already carried the only answer that would satisfy him: "Yes, he was a great soul. Men of his type are all too few."

He begged me to tell him everything I knew about

Tenko-san, and I was moved to share at least one intimacy with him. For when I met Itto-En's founder shortly before his passing some six years ago, he presented me with his one and only personal possession, an *inro* (a small pouch) with a tiny ivory skull as its *netsuke* (bit of ornamentation on the draw-string). Japanese gentlemen used to carry their most precious possession in an *inro,* a jewel, medicine, money.

Tenko-san had his most prized treasure in his *inro,* too. *Nothing.* To possess nothing was his creed, his counsel, and his faith. "In having nothing lies your most inexhaustible wealth," was his axiom. Early in life he gave away fame (he was once a member of parliament), possessions, home, family, friends, keeping only the *inro,* which he gave to me.

The long-haired youth listened with tears in his eyes. I had confirmed his secret convictions about Tenko-san and the Itto-En. Now he was sure that his deep feelings about the founder were true.

Had he never felt this way about anything or anyone in Christianity? Never. Had he never been moved or stirred by faith-in-action in his Protestant denomination? No.

He wondered whether I had ever heard how the turning point in Tenko Nishida's life came about? And if I had heard about it, would I mind if he told it to me, and would I verify the facts?

So he launched into the story, explaining how Tenko-san in his early thirties went seeking peace and joy, truth and understanding of the meaning in life. Though he had everything that should make an ordinary man content, life still seemed incomplete. Shinto,

Buddhism, Christianity, which held the answer? Tenko-san had studied them all and still wondered. Then he got hold of Tolstoi's *My Religion*. In it he found the words, "Die if you wish to live!" This, as far as Tenko Nishida was concerned, tied together what both the Buddha and the Christ had said, but how could a man die and still live to the benefit of all mankind?

Tenko-san went into a wayside Buddhist chapel to meditate on Tolstoi's words. For three days he struggled with the truth, a truth that his heart told him was right, but for which his mind could find no solution. On the morning of the fourth day he heard a baby cry down in the valley. "That," Tenko-san told himself, "is like my cry for God. Crying must be essential, for now the mother will come and both mother and child will be satisfied. So God, hearing my cry, will come to me."

That was how it happened. The child stopped crying and Tenko-san knew that its mother was feeding it and they both were happy. So he decided to exercise the same kind of faith and dependency as the little child. To all intents and purposes, he "died," leaving his worldly goods to whomever they would have been left eventually. Now people were drawn to him because he had not only found a way of life, but lived it.

Yes, that was the story of Tenko-san's conversion. He gave up his family and home and, with his wife, who had also caught his vision, began to work only for others, depending upon God for food as a child depends upon its mother for milk.

"To suck the mother's breast is not to struggle for existence," Tenko Nishida explained, "or to battle or compete against others. There is no milk before the baby is born. It is only by its birth that milk arises. The baby does not strive to gain the milk, nor does the mother strive to provide it. Both are nourished by the grace of nature."

Such was his analogy of the new birth of man and God's grace of nourishment for the newly born. Itto-En came into being when a wealthy landowner, impressed by Tenko-san's selfless life, donated twenty-five acres of land on which he could live with those who wished to follow his example of the gospel of nothingness. So a community grew, and today, as in the past, the members of the community still go to villages where help is needed and do the most menial jobs. Once they were referred to as "those lunatics who clean latrines to the glory of God," but gradually their example of living close to God won the respect of everyone. Transients are always welcome at Itto-En. They are permitted to stay one night and then move on to make a decision with their lives.

"Itto-En is not derived from any philosophy or religion," Tenko-san used to say. "It is an experiment which came into being spontaneously and independently, and I proceed only as directed by the Light. Our way of life can never be understood by the intellect. Members should never try to explain it intellectually. It can be understood only by living it."

Which is what the young man who had come under the influence of the movement intended to do, for there was as yet nothing quite like the Itto-En in the American religious scene. Itto-En is unique, but so are all of Japan's dramatically emerging faiths, some twenty major ones. All have a special, extraordinary center of appeal, tailored to capture the imagination and challenge of those who feel that the old-time religion may no longer be good enough for modern man.

3

Not all of Japan's new religions, by any means, advocate giving up one's possessions and home and family in order to be guided by the Light. On the contrary, most of them emphatically add "prosperity" to their aims for a fuller, more integrated, spiritual life. They insist that economic security inevitably follows as a natural concomitant for those who live God's will and obey God's plan.

Take the religion called Perfect Liberty, which is rapidly becoming one of the most formidable challengers for prominence among Japanese religions introduced into the United States. Its director for the expansion of the work in North America, the Rev. Koreaki Yano, has established his headquarters in Glendale, California, where he serves an active Perfect Liberty church with a staff of young and competent fellow ministers. "PL" is the only Japanese religion with an English name. When the title was announced in 1946, the leader of the movement, Patriarch Tokuchika Miki, insisted that since the work was to be international in nature, it should carry a name in a language which is also international.

Perfect Liberty is not only international, it is ultramodern. At its imposing headquarters at Tondabayashi near Osaka, we find such innovations as a computerized system of spiritual-medical healing, a peace tower as tall and commanding as the Washington Monument, golf courses with three hundred teen-aged caddies, an experimental botanical project, a fine arts center, and an educational complex for the training of ministers and missionaries dedicated to the development of the twenty-first-century man!

At first glance, all of this would seem to be the complete antithesis of Itto-En, but deep at the core of PL teaching is the same emphasis on the need for the effacement of the ego (one of its principal precepts) and at the head of its phenomenal growth stands a leader as loved and respected as any saintly Tenko-san. Self-expression is his aim, and "Life is Art" his creed. So steady has been PL's growth during the past twenty years that its membership is now pressing close to the three-million mark.

I caught the excitement of its growth when I was at Tondabayashi recently for the birthday observance of Patriarch Miki on April 8. Some 15,000 guests were on hand for the daylong ceremonies. Celebrants included delegations from foregin countries, Brazil particularly, where the work is prospering, and converts from Europe and the United States.

"This religion," a San Francisco business executive said emphatically, "speaks to me in the language of our time. It approaches situations without preconceptions. It is not bound by the past. My religion insisted on defending tradition and proving that its ancient doctrines were as valid today as they were five hundred years ago. Well, they aren't. Everything changes and religion must change. PL says that if we say, 'I know how to meet the situation,' or 'I have always believed this way, so it must be right,' we rule out creativity. I agree. We don't rule out creativity in *business*. We don't *live* the way we did five hundred years ago. Why should we keep on *thinking* the way we did? There may be better ways and better beliefs than those that were handed down to us."

The departure from stereotype can be seen in the methods employed by the Perfect Liberty Association International (PLAI). This efficient missionary outreach presents its members with a "credit card" admitting the bearer to PL golf courses, bowling alleys, fine arts seminars, and to medical services in the PL hospitals at Habikino, the Tondabayashi headquarters. The projected plan of PLAI is to establish PL community centers around the world, serving the needs of its members from the cradle to the grave. PL's specialization in child training, family relationships, and pre-school educational practices are becoming internationally recognized. Its medical services have enlisted some of Japan's finest psychiatric and psychosomatic specialists. Ministerial training includes work in the fine arts, especially in the *tanka* (a fixed form of versification), and in psychoanalysis and personal counseling. What PLAI is saying is that there must be a new "life-style" before a new world can be born, and the new life-style requires a new kind of individual.

Such is the heart of the work and the basis of PL's appeal. Up to now, says Patriarch Miki, man has stressed only the "humanness" of his nature. He has sought to prove by all means that he is a "human" being, and this has left a great deal to be desired. The time has now come for man to emphasize the "divine" in his nature, not through clichés or handy phrases as in the past, but by evidence in his life and thought that he is a manifestation of God.

Mankind, according to PL, has been moving toward this grand denouement, the advent of the God-man, since time began. Prophets have spoken of him, religions have envisioned him, the world has expected him. Now, at long last, all signs point to the fact of his imminent appearance among all nations through the awakening light of Perfect Liberty.

It has already coined its own terms for this millenial breakthrough. It calls it the "Great Peace" which the new man will usher in. The Peace Tower, dominating the 2,500 acres at PL headquarters, symbolizes the coming of this Great Peace through the concept that "Life is Art." That is why young men are being trained at Habikino not only as ministers of religion but as artists, for it is PL's belief that if we approach life as an artist approaches the material with which he works, we will better understand the technique and the qualities of the twenty-first-century man.

Contrary to Itto-En, which maintains that its beliefs should not be discussed or analyzed intellectually, PL urges that its precepts—21 of them—be tested and proved and spiritually demonstrated in every walk of life.

1. Life is Art.
2. Man's life is a succession of self-expressions.
3. Man is a manifestation of God.
4. Man suffers if he fails to express himself.

5. Man loses his true self when swayed by feelings and emotions.
6. Man's true self is revealed when his ego is effaced.
7. All things exist in mutual relationship to one another.
8. Live radiantly as the sun.
9. All men are equal.
10. Strive for creating mutual happiness.
11. Have true faith in God.
12. There is a function peculiar to every existence.
13. There is a way for men and another way for women.
14. All is for world peace.
15. All is a mirror.
16. All things progress and develop.
17. Comprehend what is most essential.
18. At every moment man stands at the crossroads of good and evil.
19. Act when your intuition dictates.
20. Live in perfect unity of mind and matter.
21. Live in Perfect Liberty.

Perfect Liberty, its members say, is ready for the world, and, one day, the world will be ready for Perfect Liberty.

4

But Perfect Liberty is by no means alone in its ambitious programming for what it believes is a waiting world. There are other new religions from the enchanted islands of Japan which are sending highly skilled missionaries to our door. There is Soka Gakkai, the incredible "Value-creating Association," which already has 30,000 members in the U.S. and whose phenomenal growth in Japan has struck concern into the hearts of critics who feel that the movement aims at national political control.

The teachings of this fast-moving faith are so authoritarian that an American mother wrote me in despair that her teen-aged son was "a captive under the influence of this foreign faith." Even the name "Soka Gakkai" frightened her, she said, and she had no doubt its power was hypnotic. Her son, however, insisted that now for the first time he knew what religion truly meant, and as far as he was concerned Soka Gakkai was the most humane and logical of all beliefs.

The membership of this controversial organization has been put at fifteen million, with an estimate that this figure involves some five million Japanese families. It is politically potent. Nineteen of its candidates have been elected to the National Diet. It wields powerful labor influences and has been accused by equally powerful labor unions, notably Tanro, the coal miners' union, of being ruthless and exploitive in its aims. It is so tightly knit and so dominantly controlled by its group of leaders that it has been difficult for outsiders to learn all about the inner operations of this modern expression of Japanese Buddhism.

I came close to a feeling about Soka Gakkai when, after considerable investigation of my intentions, the officials admitted me to one of their festivals. The observance was held in the outdoor stadium built for the

Tokyo Olympics. A hundred thousand Soka Gakkai enthusiasts were in the stands. Five thousand young men of the Value-creating Society marched in military style on the sunlit grounds carrying Nichiren banners and chanting Nichiren sutras.

Nichiren Daishonin, Soka Gakkai's patron saint, was a dedicated Buddhist monk of the thirteenth century, whose impassioned teaching in his day was a foretaste of what Soka Gakkai's principles and practices are now. Nichiren also agitated for the spiritualization of national life by every possible means: through politics, labor, education, industry, the home, and the masses. That is Soka Gakkai's aim today. As one member remarked to me, "First Japan, then America, and when America— the world!"

Interestingly enough, many American converts have come from among GIs who were doing military duty in Japan. One of these, William MacDougall of San Francisco, told the press how the faith is being propagated.

"First we make friends," he said, "people we meet at work. We ask them to our home, show them Soka Gakkai literature, and then invite them to a meeting. You see, we believe in the search for happiness, and we can only find it by getting into harmony with life here and now. We do not emphasize the hereafter, It is *now,* here in our life, that we must change."

Soka Gakkai's third president, Daisaku Ikeda, added a classical touch to the propagation of the faith when he said, "We are engaged in spreading the religion abroad because we consider it as a mission entrusted to us for the sake of world peace. Going back 2,000 years it will be recalled that Christianity made a vast contribution

111

to mankind. As if in reaction, communism is now posing a serious menace to the world. The Hegelian dialectic, which moves from thesis to antitheses to synthesis, explains how our faith has resulted from this reaction. We are trying our best, and we consider it our duty to spread our faith to other countries in the belief that it can be helpful in solving the world's trouble."

Meetings are usually held in private homes in Soka Gakkai's American program, and here the ritual prayers are recited and the principles of the faith are discussed. The appeal is largely to youth and the training is skillfully balanced so that body, mind, and spirit have their synthesized programming.

"The way of youth is the way of the world," says Soka Gakkai, "and that is why we train young members for leadership both in the theoretical study of Buddhism and in the practical propagation of this supreme religion. We mean the youth of every land because Nichiren Daishonin had in mind the salvation of the world. The new convert should therefore know exactly how to save those who do not understand just what Nichiren Buddhism actually is."

And what is it?

It is, as has been said, a religion of absolute authority, hierarchical testimony based on Saint Nichiren, who considered himself the reincarnation of the true Buddha. As compared with Perfect Liberty and other new faiths which find affinity with the great religions of the world, Soka Gakkai is rigidly exclusive.

"Except in mysterious legends of the past," says the official pronouncement, "most of the religions in the world have lost the power to grant men's wishes. Only the religion of Nichiren Daishonin holds the great power to answer the prayers of mankind. This is not, however, the limit of the wonder. Not only are prayers answered, but there is a redevelopment of one's character, reforming one's personality unawares while worshiping the *gohonzon* (object of worship)."

Its promises are unlimited. "During the time a man is still in this world he will acquire the vital life-force and fortune to enable him to overcome every obstacle in life. He will also come to realize the happiness of the next life and to realize that life is eternal. This great divine favor, this ultimate purpose of believing, is called *jobutsu*. Its concept has no comparison with that found in other religions. Christianity calls the hardships of life 'trials from God,' making its followers believe in a heaven which can never be proved scientifically. All religions in the world are powerless to solve or satisfy the problem of worldly passions and desire. But the benefits of *jobutsu*, taught by Nichiren Daishonin, are the ultimate and supreme happiness, both material and spiritual, a state that will never die, no matter what the situation."

Thus, according to Soka Gakkai, Nichiren established the law, revealed the final truth, and though he lived in the thirteenth century (1222-82), he never really died. His life and spirit continued in the devotion of his followers. It was not until 1930, however, that the modern interpretation of Nichiren appeared through the inspired writings of a schoolmaster, Makiguchi Tsunesaburo, who founded the Value-creating Society in Tokyo in 1937.

The big publicity that drew attention to the movement (as was also the case with other emerging religions in Japan) came in 1943 when Makiguchi was arrested, along with twenty of his followers, on charges of blasphemy against Emperor Hirohito. Makiguchi died while in solitary confinement, and it remained for one of his imprisoned confreres, Josei Toda, to assume leadership following his own release from prison at the end of the war. In 1952, following Toda's death, the leadership passed to Daisaku Ikeda.

However, the actual power is not in leadership alone, but in the *Gohonzon,* a written scroll inscribed by Nichiren Daishonin in 1279. Mystically, it refers to the life and spirit of the saint, say the followers, and practically, it answers people's needs and imparts the life-force through the praying of *Nam-myoho-renge-kyo.* The meaning of these words is deeply symbolic and filled with many esoteric connotations. Simply stated, they mean the recognition of life as divine life and the discovery within oneself of the qualities personified in St. Nichiren.

Understandably, the mother who wrote me about her son who had joined Soka Gakkai based her concern in part, at least, on the tirades of this brash and booming faith against Christianity. Though it has mellowed somewhat, here are several excerpts from its earlier literature,

Jesus worked miracles. They say that forty-six miracles have been put on record. However, posterity could have invented these miracles. They cannot be proven just by the fact that they are written in the Bible. Even nowadays Christians call all sorts of unusual phenomena miracles. It betrays their inferiority that they are ignorant of the reason behind these phenomena.

Jesus died on the Cross. This shows that he was defeated by opposition, whatever interpretation posterity may have given to this fact. Our great Saint Nichiren shouted to his executor when he was about to be beheaded: "The time is passing. Be quick! Cut off my head!" And as soon as he said so, the gods of the universe gave him all the power of their protection, and meteors shot across the heavens. *He* defeated his opposition. Comparing this vitality with the fate of Jesus, we see that Christianity has no power.

—(Shakufuku Kyoten 1954)

Nonetheless, as the American converts gather for worship, removing their shoes and kneeling before the *Gohonzon,* as they reverently press their palms together and chant, *"Nam-myoho-renge-kyo,"* they feel themselves part of a movement that demands their loyalty and commands their total dedication. But, after all, to the faithful who work and study and serve, Soka Gakkai has promised that,

> No prayer is unanswered,
> No sin unforgiven;
> All good fortune will be bestowed,
> And righteousness will be proven.

5

Obviously Soka Gakkai is something of a maverick in the field of these new and prospering faiths, for the phenomenon in the dramatic rise of Japanese religions generally is their emphasis on peace and joy and their spirit of *camaraderie* and ecumenical goodwill. It is as if they sincerely recognized the validity of each one's particular expression and the divine right of specific revelations. Their attitude also seems to indicate that Japan is large enough and the need of the world is great enough to permit each movement to put its products into the open market. A Gamaliel-type attitude is part of their approach, "If this counsel or this work be of men, it will come to nought: But if it be of God, ye cannot overthrow it!" (Acts 5:38-39)

So the revival and expansion continue at an amazing pace.

In Tokyo we find that Rissho Koseikai (Society for Righteousness and Cordial Interrelationship) is becoming a mecca for tourists who have heard of its phenomenal growth and find it difficult to believe the reports on hearsay. Founded in 1938, Rissho Koseikai conservatively estimates its membership at 2,800,000. Seeing is believing, as I discovered in my visits to its headquarters at No. 27 Wadahonmachi, Suginami-ku. Here stands its Grand Temple, by far the largest religious building in the Orient, comfortably accommodating 50,000. It contains complete facilities for feeding a multitude of this size and rises seven stories to a tiered and towering dome dominating an incredible rooftop of pure copper.

On an ordinary weekday at any hour, five to fifteen thousand people gather for worship and spiritual sharing. They call these gatherings *hoza,* or "family circle groups," and the object is a series of counseling sessions with sensitivity overtones. The program is well-named when it speaks of family participation, because the emphasis in Rissho Koseikai is strongly on family life and interfamily relationships. *Hoza* provides an opportunity for open discussions of problems, resolving of difficulties and instruction in the faith. What is aimed at, however, is "the attainment of perfect personality" or "Buddhahood through the development of one's own inner Buddha nature."

Rissho Koseikai, a Nichiren-inspired movement, is considerably more joyful and benign than Soka Gakki. A friend of mine, "Joe" Kamomiya, Director of Doctrinal Research, could never, in my judgment, be a member of anything but Rissho Koseikai. He has a joyful, outward-going spirit and an instinctive dedication to this highly democratic faith. Neither he nor his superiors ever seek to impose a psychological distance between themselves and their people. The reason, Kamomiya made clear to me, is that all of us are involved in the karmic process, the inexorable law of cause and effect. Each person is working out his destiny and is caught in a chain of circumstances which demands divine mercy and knowledge and understanding. So why should the "spirit of mortal be proud," or set itself above its fellowman?

But for its Buddhistic adherence, Rissho Koseikai has a terminology well understood by conservative Christians. It is all there: repentance, restitution, redemption, salvation. The difference, beyond the fact that the Buddha takes the place of Christ, lies in the doctrine of reincarnation, always a coordinate with the Karmic law. If man truly desires to enter eternal life, he needs time. He needs *lifetimes*. And this is what Rissho Koseikai promises: time for the attainment of spiritual perfection and eternal bliss through a series of rebirths.

I was at Rissho Koseikai for the festival day of Nichiren (October 12). Those who accompanied me

117

still speak of the spectacular pageantry of the floats and parades which went on far into the night, and even more of the absolute joy and disciplined revelry that dominated the devotees. The revered leader of the movement, Niwano Nikkyo, was present, both as spectator and participant. The countless thousands who shared in the celebration were predominantly from Japan's middle and working classes, and women were far in the majority. But the appeal of Rissho Koseikai in its efficient and practical solving of social and personal dilemmas has already established itself among Americans of Japanese descent on our west coast and in metropolitan centers where it is beginning to be known as the religion that keeps families together by ministering to family concerns.

6

Tenrikyo, religion of Heavenly Wisdom, is also crowding the three million mark in membership and is one of the oldest of the "new religions" gaining western attention. Headquartered in the heart of Tenri City, whose nearly 100,000 citizens are almost without exception Heavenly Wisdom members, Tenrikyo is a highly eclectic faith. It recognizes the practical features of Shinto which gave Tenrikyo birth, it includes Buddhist teachings which have contributed to its philosophy, and it has adapted many of the moral and ethical teachings of Christianity.

While at Tenrikyo I was convinced that the report was true: a thousand missionaries are being readied to carry the gospel of *Yokigurashi* (Joy in God) into all the world. Some of these enthusiastic advocates are already in America teaching people the sacred dances and the fascinating mimetic prayers of a religion which believes it will someday be the universally accepted faith of all mankind. Such was the promise and the vision of the foundress, Nakayama Miki, who a century ago proclaimed herself to be the incarnation of the "true and original God." To those who dared cavil at such presumption, the untutored Miki adroitly presented a series of canonical writings, including the seventeen books of Tenrikyo scriptures, the *Ofudesaki,* containing the doctrines of salvation.

Inherent in the teaching are several unique approaches to age-old truths. One is the idea of custodianship, the warning that everything one is and possesses is merely a loan from God. This impressed itself upon me as I recalled that, in my early catechetical instruction in the German Reformed Church, one of our first memorized principles was, "My only comfort in life and in death is that I am not my own, but belong to my faithful Savior Jesus Christ." The words flashed back to me at Tenri. Tenrikyo teaching put it more pointedly than I had learned it. It said, "To act as if our own bodies and all that we possess is our property breaks the harmony and order that exists between man and the universe. If we betray the truth that all is loaned us, God will warn us by sending sickness and other adversities."

A second graphic concept involves the analogy of dust and sin. Evil, offense against God, and the seven deadly sins (Tenrikyo lists eight: anger, greed, parsimony, lust, hatred, covetousness, animosity, and arrogance), are dust on our soul and result in the scattering of dust over all the world. This symbolic reference goes deep into the lives of believers and makes visual an otherwise obscure and theologically involved teaching of the nature of sin. Tenrikyo believes that dust (sin) is removed by an acknowledgment of the custodial principle and by enacting the famous *Tenri-o-no-mikoto* prayer. This is a mimetic worship to "God the Parent," a chant to the accompaniment of *kotos* and the great gong. Rhythmic hand movements pantomime the hypnotic cadences which say in effect, "We sweep the dust of evil from our souls! We fill our souls with thy love and joy!"

As a reminder that the body is the temple of God and must be continually cleansed, so the great temple at Tenri is dusted and scoured each day. Hundreds of volunteers get down on their knees and do the furbishing to the accompaniment of sacred work songs. This, incidentally, is also the cooperative technique by which the roads and museums, libraries and schools of Tenrikyo were built, by volunteers singing at their work, devotees who come to Tenri from Tenrikyo's 20,000 branch churches, making their pilgrimage to their holy city, experiencing *yokugurashi,* Joy in God.

There are also sufficient mystical features in Tenrikyo to enthrall the most fastidious worshiper and cause him to speak in awed terms about apocalyptic promises. For example, though the foundress died at the ripe old age of 90, she had predicted she would live to be 115, an age which all people will attain after the coming of *kanro,* the "sweet dew of heaven" which marks the advent of the new age.

There is at Tenrikyo a hexagonal wooden column some nine feet high, bearing on its top an open wooden receptacle which is supposed to catch the first "sweet dew," then overflow and flood the Sanctuary of the Foundress situated nearby. It is actually a dwelling where, it is believed, the discarnate spirit of Nakayama Miki still lives and awaits the coming of her prophecy. Priestly attendants reverently do guard duty night and day at the entrance to this building, and faithful zealots bring food daily to the spirit presence. The sanctuary is kept spotlessly free from dust, and various comforts, including a television set, are provided in the assurance that their unseen guest is comfortable while awaiting the inevitable coming of the millenniar day and the promise of the showering of the heavenly sweet dew, the mystic *kanro*.

Meantime, too, there is a daily *kanrodai* dance performed unseen by any spectators. Ten masked participants perform a cosmic choreography depicting the birth of the world, the creation of man, and the destiny of mankind under the watchful eye of God the Parent. Though no one sees the wonder of this performance, the sounds are heard as the shuffling feet stir up the small round pebbles which have been scattered over the dancing area. And with this, too, it is believed, the Foundress is well pleased.

7

Because English-speaking people found it difficult to pronounce and to understand Seikai Kyusei Kyo, or Nippon Kannon Kyodan, the religion founded by Okada

Mokichi in 1934, the name has recently been popularized as World Messianity. To the Japanese this has become as acceptable as its native equivalent: Seikai Meshiya Kyo. Okada anglicized the name because he was eager to attract followers of all countries and all faiths, particularly American Christians. He felt they would understand the revelation that came to him when God proclaimed him a new messiah with special healing in his hands. After all, Christians knew about these things. They had accepted a Messiah 2,000 years ago and he, too, had performed his healing miracles. Naturally they would be attracted to Okada Mokichi.

As for the Buddhists, they too should by all means be drawn to him. The Buddha had performed miracles and had surrounded himself with disciples who had seen evidences of supernatural happenings. Furthermore, in one of Okada's revelations, he had been told he was the incarnation of Kannon, Buddhist Goddess of Mercy. And since he had come out of the Omoto religion, which had its Shinto roots, there was no reason to doubt that World Messianity would be the religion that all people had been secretly seeking and hopefully waiting to appear.

But the greatest of Okada's revelations was the clearcut vision he had of *jorei,* the healing light which possessed him with igniting force and emanated from the palm of his hand. In early Christian times, as Mokichi understood it, the Apostles had blessed kerchiefs and cloths and had employed magical incantations which contained curative powers. He too had this art. He could write the word *hikari* (light) in a special way on a special type of paper and if a person placed this on his place of ache or pain, he would be cured. He had countless testimonies to prove this claim, and people had paid him well for services rendered. So well, in fact, that he had become a rich man, wealthier by far than he had ever been when he was in the brokerage business or dealing in stocks and bonds.

His most persuasive evidence of divine power, he always felt, was his own longevity. Born in 1882, he was at his healthiest best in the early 1950's when Messianity and he were building two utopian settlements, one in the Hakone mountains and the other on a promontory overlooking Atami Bay. He proclaimed that a man could live unlimitedly and that there was nothing that *jorei* and *hikari* could not heal. But he wasted away in prison on a tax-evasion charge and died there at the age of 73.

The reputation and achievement of Okada Mokichi was such, however, that despite his untimely demise, his followers not only honored him with one of the most lavish funerals Japan has ever seen, but increased in number and devotion to his teaching after he was gone. His theories were always exciting and many of his accomplished cures were too spectacular to be written off as merely imaginary or psychological in nature.

Modern metaphysicians who have frequently referred to the soul as "the ether of the universe" found Okada's concepts not at all farfetched. Contending that the element which fills all space is a divine force upon which all things depend for health and growth, he identified the essence of this power with *jorei*. A person who could consolidate *jorei* and learn how to transmit it to another person or thing was unquestionably a co-worker with God in the healing of the world.

The power he claimed for himself he taught to others, instructing them how to discover, develop, and use the *jorei* emanation. I saw it demonstrated when I visited the Messianity headquarters at Atami, and though there was no way to prove the authenticity of the purported cures (doctors are not consulted or involved in any of the experiments), there was no doubting the sincerity and commitment of the practitioners. They had passed their course of study in the use of *jorei* and were wearing the concealed talisman, a charm with the word *hikari* on a chain around their necks, much as a believing Catholic wears the Agnus Dei or another religious medal. The *hikari* emblem, it is believed, localizes the *jorei* and when the practitioner properly focuses the palm of his hand on the patient, the divine healing ray dispels disease and eases pain.

The surroundings at Atami were of such beauty and magnificence that, as far as setting was concerned, the utopian ideal seemed well within reach. Here the followers of Okada have established a museum housing exquisite Nipponese art, acclaimed by critics as among the rarest treasures in Japan. The museum is open to the public in galleries that radiate a profoundly spiritual atmosphere. The libraries and study halls are also in excellent decor. When I commented on the attractively landscaped grounds, I was informed by my Messianity companion that *jorei* is directed not only at the purification and healing of human life but is concentrated upon the soil as well.

Many Japanese farmers, he informed me, are numbered among Messianity's half million members. You will find no chemical fertilizer, or fertilizer of any kind, used on their farms, he assured me. Instead there are ceremonies for blessing the land and honoring the elements, and invoking the sun which is, to many, the *jorei* of the universe, wearing the talisman of cosmic light.

This, too, is part of the testimony told by World Messianity's missionaries as they proceed to bring the teachings and techniques of Okada Mokichi to our door.

8

The religion known as Konkokyo takes its name from a revelation that came to a farmer in a field near Konko City in Okayama Prefecture. The date of the vision that changed the life of farmer Kawate Bunjiro in 1859 hardly justifies Konkokyo as an emerging faith, but the influence it currently wields in the areas of world peace and in the ecumenical approach to religion makes it one of the most important and progressive of the new and expanding movements of Japan. One of its emissaries, the Rev. Toshio Miyake, pastor of the thriving Konkokyo work in Osaka, is internationally important in every world conference on religion and peace. In 1970 he was one of the host pastors in the Kyoto meetings sponsored by the Methodist Division of World Peace.

The ecumenical impact of Konkokyo is now beginning to be realized, and the long reach of the history of this unique faith is being talked about and studied by American scholars as the converging relationship of

Christian and non-Christian efforts directs itself to the challenges of our time.

How could it all have started with a farmer's vision? The obvious answer is: commitment and devotion, together with a practical basis for making religion meaningful in the individual life. For Kawate Bunjiro's experience was by no means unusual in the anthology of Japanese faiths. Like Nakayama Miki of Tenrikyo, like Ogamisama of the "Dancing Religion" (Tensho Kotai Jungu Kyo), or like Masaharu Taniguchi, founder of the intensely popular Seicho No Ie, Bunjiro felt he had a visitation from "God the Parent" and found himself under orders. But his God was special and identified himself as *Tenchi-kane-no-kami.* From that moment on, Bunjiro took the spiritual name, *Konko Daijin,* which meant the manifestation on earth of the one true God.

The dominant note in his experience was "joy and prosperity." A unique feature was the recognition that, as man depends upon God, so God is also dependent upon man. An innovation was the practice of *toritsugi,* a form of confessional-counseling in which the minister plays the part of mediator between God and the worshiper.

The dramatic aspect of *toritsugi* was impressed upon me during my stay at Konkokyo headquarters where the grandson of the founder, Konko Setsutane, was serving as patriarch of the faith. An elderly man and quite incapacitated, he still maintained the vigil he had followed for more than sixty years. Daily for more than half a century he had gone to the sanctuary at six in the morning, taken his place on a prayer mat, and remained there meditating and mediating until sundown.

People came to him daily to make their confessions and elicit his counsel.

I was reminded of the deep sincerity of Konko Setsutane when I recently shared in the dedication of a great new temple of the Konkokyo Church at Izuo, Osaka. The thousands who came to this event typified the qualities of courtesy, devotion, and spiritual understanding which are the hallmarks of the leaders of this faith, and which were so characteristic of the patriarch.

Konkokyo's daily services (the first at six in the morning) could, to all intents and purposes, be held in any liberal Protestant church. Gospel songs with words and music reminiscent of Christian hymns, the prayers, the sermon, the atmosphere of freedom and informality, would all be familiar to a Protestant worshiper. The difference of course, besides the language factor, would be theological. There is emphasis on Jesus, but not on the Christ as "Savior," and the God is Tenchi-kane-no-kami. This God also inspired the erstwhile untutored farmer to write the Konkokyo Scriptures, a series of sacred admonitions and precepts which, better than theological doctrines, give insight into the grace and gentility of this expanding movement:

It is no miracle at all that God's blessing is given in answer to prayer. It would indeed be a miracle if it were not given.

Faith polishes the jewel of your heart.

A believer should be sincere in all things.

When you see the immoral conduct of others, beware of following into their evil ways.

Pray for your physical health and build up a healthy body, which is the source of all the blessings of life.

Harmony in the home is the foundation of faith.

Your training in faith consists, not in any form of mortification, but in the sincere pursuit of your daily occupations.

The heart that sympathizes with others is a godly heart.

Since we are all children of God, no one is a stranger to us.

Be not narrow-minded in your faith. Think of the world with a broad mind, for the world does exist in your mind.

The simplicity of Konkokyo is part of its charm. Its teachings tell us we have forgotten God. In our forgetting we suffer and God suffers with us. Our sorrow is God's sorrow. God wishes to save us, but his grace is wasted if we resist his will. Let us, therefore, listen to Konko Daijin, for God sent him to clarify things, to mediate between us and God, and pave the way for our salvation.

All of which may just be simple and sincere enough to make us pause and reflect, as Konkokyo missionaries begin to probe the western world to test our response to their uncomplicated faith.

As we have said, in these and other new religions of Japan, the pattern is the same: unquestioned dedication to the leaders and the cause, unlimited cooperation in the plans for expansion, unquestioned and uncritical trust in the teachings.

And, as we have also pointed out, to understand the psychology involved in such devotion it is necessary to take a backward glance to the time a short quarter century ago when a new God was born because an old god had died.

6

Togetherness

1

Among the strangest of the strangers at our door is a self-styled Korean seer name Sun Myung Moon. I met him for the first time in 1965 in Washington, D.C., when a friend of mine, Arthur Ford, the noted psychic, was also present at an informal house reception for the forty-five-year-old visitor from Seoul. Later Mr. Ford was to report on several trance sessions with Mr. Moon and write about him at length in his book *Unknown But Known*. On this occasion, however, the impact of the meeting was considerably more psychological than psychic.

What impressed me most was not any message channeled through Mr. Ford, but, rather, the undisputed devotion which some forty or fifty young Korean and American followers displayed for the pensive Mr. Moon, whose homespun philosophy was by no means new and whose arguments were hardly convincing. Yet, one of the young men told me during a peripatetic stroll that he was convinced that Sun Myung Moon was the promised Messiah whom all religions had foretold. He was the Second Coming. This conviction, I was to learn later, was considerably more contagious than I would possibly have guessed.

When I say that Mr. Moon's preachment through his interpreters and by way of his translated writings held nothing innovative, I mean that he was of the opinion that America needed saving, that its people are not living up to the standard of the Christian life, and that we are far from being the kind of spiritually dedicated human beings that God wants us to be.

This was hardly news. Nor was it extraordinary that Sun Moon wished to save us. Our own evangelists have been wanting to do this for generations, and a host of offshore missionaries, as we have seen, are currently dedicated to the same proposition. Perhaps we are becoming inured to this vicarious concern. It may be that we feel it is often a ploy for building up large and thriving organizations and using the high-powered commercialized media for playing upon the sentimentality of faith which slumbers deep within us vagrant westerners. At any rate, both Christian and non-Christian prophets have been quick to adopt the Madison Avenue method for selling us their gospel fare.

Mr. Moon made it clear at this first house-party meeting that his heart was burdened because we Americans did not appreciate our blessings. He was convinced that heaven is holding untold riches for us if we will but show ourselves worthy to receive them. We may feel we are an affluent nation, but we have no idea how affluent we could be if we but took God at his word. Mr. Moon told us he loved us so much that he had come to us in tears to show us where we have erred. He had such faith in us that he was willing to point out to us where our faith has gone astray. He anguished for us and said,

"I did not come to the United States as tourist or sightseer. Immediately upon arriving, I prayed that I might take up the burden to relieve God of the greatest problem of the United States. I traveled through each and every one of the forty-eight continental states in forty days. In fact, my heart was willing to step upon the ground of every state in just twenty-one days. I told my heart that I must work harder than anyone else in the entire United States, that while others may sleep I may not, and that I will take the burden from God's heart. And even now, in an unprecedented manner, I want to love this country more than any American has ever loved it before. I am not doing this just for Americans or America, but because God, our Father, has been shedding his tears and blood for this land for many centuries. Knowing his heart and his labors, I cannot avoid taking up the burden."

This, of course, was nothing more or less than our Del Rio, Texas, radio preachers had been telling us ever since the first salvation-by-air broadcast pierced the skyways, and the only singularity about this latest approach was that we were hearing it in Korean.

Nor were the Sun Moon suppositions unique. "In the original ideal of God's creation," we were told, "God created man's mind and body as the closest of friends, united as one in a subject-object relationship and living harmoniously together. But because of the fall of man, the two closest friends are separated. The greater the distance between one's mind and body, the greater is the agony of that person's life, and as that agony increases, the social agony, the national agony, and the world agony is developed."

This exposition on the divided self was hardly original and Mr. Moon admitted it when he said, "In a sense, all of the founders of the great religions of the world have been working toward the goal of uniting mind and body. Unless you first find the unity of mind and body within yourself, no matter how you encounter divinity, it will be of no use. You can find no other source of peace until you find peace within yourself. Hence, the purpose of God's dispensation, as well as the purpose of Jesus' mission, is to unite your mind and body into one harmonious unit."

He called his missionary effort the Divine Principle movement, and certain capable amanuenses were already hard at work preparing the scriptures and tenets of its faith. One of these, Miss Young Oon Kim, student of comparative religions and a former teacher at Ewha Women's University in Seoul, was beginning to devote more and more of her time to the movement, convinced, she said, that God himself had chosen Sun Myung Moon as his contemporary revealer. I would have guessed that Miss Kim would be the most qualified interpreter for whatever the movement might hold for the western world.

After the initial Washington meeting, however, I had a feeling that the Divine Principle movement could

never, by any stretch of its imaginative wings, get off
the ground. It was too obvious in its intentions and too
complex in its "theology." As an emerging religion it
would not have the impact, say, of Subud, the Indone-
sian faith, or the fascination paid to the work of Gurdjieff, the Russian mystic whose presence had passed
with legendary force across the world.

But then came Arthur Ford's book, and people were
saying that America's foremost psychic had verified the
divine mission of a Korean sage. The Divine Principle
movement claimed that Ford's spirit-control had put
his stamp of approval on Sun Myung Moon as the
promised prophet of the Aquarian Age. A book by Miss
Kim, *Divine Principle,* carried on its jacket flap the Ford
quotation, "Out of your country, Korea, will come a
new spiritual urge. It will be a blending of the ancient
with a new revelation and it is not far off, it is near."

Supporting this pronouncement was a Divine Principle movement brochure, *A New Prophet for a New
Age,* which drew upon the out-of-context views of
scientists (Teilhard de Chardin and Lecomte du
Nouy), a churchman (Eugene Carson Blake), a political
leader (President Nixon), a clairvoyant (Edgar Cayce),
and used them as supporting evidence of the teachings
of South Korea's emissary. Soon letters came to me in-
dicating more than casual curiosity in the Divine Principle movement and quoting the Ford trance-transcrip-
tions with such enthusiasm that I got to wondering
whether Sun Myung Moon was actually any stranger
than other strangers at our door.

The movement, though still known by its Divine
Principle emphasis, began to operate under the impos-

ing title of "The Holy Spirit Association for the Unification of World Christianity," with headquarters at 1611 Upshur Street, N.W. in the capital city. It also implemented its teachings in a sociological experiment called "the Unified Family," which several of my acquaintances became interested in. The "Family" was a venture in communal or collectivistic living, dedicated to purity of heart, strict sex regulations, and an intensive study program enshrined in fellowship. It came at a time when the hip-culture was turning toward togetherness and when the street people were ready to come inside.

It was at this point that the odyssey of a friend of mine aroused my interest in a more reflective look at the dramatic denouement of Sun Myung Moon as his new planet rose in our religious skies.

2

My friend Lee Pfaff is an American Caucasian in his late twenties, a spiritual vagabond who has run an indulgent gamut from parental Pentecostalism to metaphysical Unity without finding a permanent spiritual home. The reason? Fixed in his mind was the conviction that Jesus was soon to return to earth in some dramatic way, and Lee could find no religious group that was seriously concerned with this momentous event.

Lee's mother had her own idea about the Second Advent. "Jesus is coming back," she told her son, "make no mistake about it. The social, religious, and political conditions of the world are just what they were when he came for the first time. And today, just as when he came that first time, the masses, including the churches, are going to miss him because he won't come in the way they are expecting him to come."

How was he coming? She could not say, but the thought she left lingering in Lee's heart was that the Second Coming would be more subtle than biblical promises about clouds of glory or the modern extremists' proposal that he will come swooping down in a UFO. More than likely, Lee thought, Jesus would come as a thief in the night or as another babe wrapped in swaddling clothes, to be discovered only by those who have the inner eye to see.

Lee's unquenchable quest brought him naturally enough to Los Angeles. He came longhaired and hippie-bearded and tried to locate a job in the one field, advertising, for which he had been trained. He was a qualified layout and idea man, and he tramped to various church headquarters inquiring about work and showing them what he had done for Unity and other denominations in the midwest. Religion on the California coast was different. One of the first questions he was asked was, "Are you one of us?" Actually, he wasn't. He was no longer strictly Pentecostal or Methodist or Nazarene or Vedanta or Unity or even denominationally identifiable, which may have been philosophically sound but was vocationally nonproductive. Nonetheless, he free-lanced, managed to live at the "Y," and was able to keep body and soul together as he continued his self-styled researching of what was actually happening along Church Street in Greater Los Angeles.

He wrote me at the time that, "All the religions I encounter have valuable, meaningful beliefs, but they are stagnant, encumbered with tradition, and limited in their outreach. They seem like dying religions for dying people. They have lost the vision and vitality of youth."

Over a luncheon table he told me, "In my visits to various religious services, I could only find significant numbers of young people in the ultrafundamental churches, the Oriental groups, or in scientology. I feel I have outgrown the fears and do-nots of fundamentalism. The Oriental religions didn't measure up to my concept of a balanced, meaningful life; and the always-smiling, glassy-eyed youth of scientology disturbed me with a hypnotic feeling of the unreal."

Always there was Jesus or the hope for him, and Lee's deep-dyed sense of surety about the Second Coming. He knew, of course, that every age in history had its "wars and rumors of wars" and other signs to fit any apocalyptic timetable, and that some prophetic voice from the time of Montanus to Charles Taze Russell had raised the cry of Armageddon and the Lord's return within the framework of his time.

But today with Vietnam dragging on, and pornography and blue movies, and crime in the streets, to say nothing of man daring to step into space—God's special province—and the A-bomb—Satan's ace-in-the-hole—it *did* seem that the time of the end was imminent. Jesus was undoubtedly coming, but who cared?

Then one day, while on a temporary job in an advertising agency, Lee met a girl who worked near him and who seemed to sense his spiritual concern. She told him about a religion she had found called "the Unified Family," which seemed to her the "perfect faith." Lee was skeptical, but since the girl and another member of the "Family," a young man Lee's age, proposed they take him to a service, he consented to go. His skepticism increased when they drew up before an unpretentious two-story frame building at 429 South Virgil. It looked more like a rooming house than a church, but Lee hid his misgivings.

Then he noticed, just outside the door, a large array of shoes, all shapes and sizes and of varying quality. Following the example of his companions, he placed his shoes among the others, and as he did so he had a reassuring inner response. Something said to him, "This is what the disciples did in Jesus' time." So thinking, and overcome with a deep nostalgia for a togetherness with Christians who might conceivably share his mood, he went inside.

In the large main room, the longing for fellowship increased as he saw a group of some seventy young people in their early twenties, happy, smiling, normal-looking young people who reminded him of those he had known in Bible college prayer groups. At one end of the room a group was gathered around a lecturer who used a blackboard and diagrams to illustrate "God's relationship with man." A glance at the spherical drawings revealed to Lee that in this religious movement, whatever it was, God was not in a position between subject and object, but was one with the subject at the very center of the universe.

He cocked his ears to hear the speaker say, "God created Adam to play the role of God's representative to Eve. This couple, Adam and Eve, took the role of God's representative to creation. All mankind was henceforth to be the subject and center of things. Thus man, the unified body of male and female, is at the head of the universe. Human society should also be an hierarchical organism with one center."

He joined the listening group. Some things about the Unified Family teachings sounded strangely involved, but there was no doubt about the quality and spirit of the devotees. These people, he decided, were clean-cut without being glassy-eyed. There was a healthy sense of *camaraderie* that really turned Lee on. He felt an aura of the mystical, as if there were hidden secrets no one would quite divulge and a presence no one was willing to reveal until you were in the in-group. If there was any doubt about this it was dispelled when he was caught up in the high-powered songfest featuring music written by members of the Unified Family movement.

> Gonna build a kingdom on this sad old ground;
> Gonna build a kingdom all around!
> Gonna call it heaven 'cause that's what it'll be,
> A place of beauty, peace and joy for you and me.
>
> It'll take a struggle, but we'll see it through,
> Go and tell your friends if they want to come,
> That they're all welcome to this land we call
>   freedom!
>
> Fight determined to be victors, and we'll ease
>   this pain for men,
> We've a kingdom to establish with our tears, our
>   sweat, our blood;
> And we'll kick to hell this world of hell, and
>   build a new world for God!

So come all you people, it's your kingdom, too;
'Cause it won't be a kingdom without you.
So rejoice my brothers, all men of all lands;
For the glory of the true world—that wonderful
  me and you world—
That kingdom of the new world is at hand!

Behind the songs and the happy time was the deep and serious business of "religion at work." The Unified Family was the product of the Unification Church, and the Unification Church was based on the *Divine Principle* and its application in the life of man, providing, according to both the publicity and the teaching, "a breakaway from evil and sorrow by becoming a better person, renewing the understanding of your purpose, your involvement, your complete existence by looking at it from a new direction and with a very new point of view."

For Lee, who had grown up with the apocalyptic promises of Pentecostalism, there was nothing unusual in the undertone of excitement that Jesus was coming again, except that these followers of Sun Myung Moon spoke of the new dispensation as if the Second Coming had already been *fulfilled*. And as Lee dug deeper into the texts of the *Divine Principle,* he realized that, though it was never explicitly stated, it was certainly implicitly implied that the Lord of the second Advent was none other than Mr. Moon himself. The telltale inferences were there and all that was needed was for someone to proclaim, "This, in truth, is he!"

This was part of the aura and a good deal of the mystique that moved through the members of the Unified Family. To think of being part of the chosen band who were in on the secret recognition was enough to make anyone feel he was among the elect. For those who took this seriously, as Lee did, it was like finding a pearl of great price and jealously guarding it against unnecessary polemics and unbelief. Nonetheless, he began asking more and more questions about Sun Myung Moon and was not surprised to find ready-made romances and almost legendary accounts surrounding this mystery man of Korea.

At the age of sixteen, so the story went, Sun Myung Moon experienced a vision on a bright and shining Easter morn. Jesus appeared to him and imparted the verbal message that God was preparing Sun Moon for a universal mission.

"From then on," said the account in the *Divine Principle,* "Mr. Moon's spiritual senses were fully opened, enabling him to communicate with the highest realms of the spirit world. He, however, did not content himself merely with the demonstration of spiritual phenomena. He began to explore the hidden meanings of the parables and symbols in the Bible and the fundamental concepts and questions of Christianity and other religions."

In short, the "ultimate view of life and the universe" was revealed to Sun Myung Moon as it had never, according to Divine Principle followers, been expounded or exposed to any man. Later Sun Moon was to say in a lecture titled, "The Master Speaks on the Lord of the Second Advent," "When you read the Bible, it appears as if Jesus knew everything. But he didn't. He did not know how the fall of man took place as clearly as we do. He did not comprehend the history of restoration.

The Lord to come is the King of Wisdom and the Prince of Love!"

The members of the Unified Family believed this almost without question. They had come from various byways of life, drawn by the magnet of prophecy fulfilled. One of the members who greatly impressed Lee was an erstwhile Lutheran from Wisconsin. Three years ago he had left his family to roam through hippiedom in a search for self, and claimed that, when he encountered the Divine Principle people in Arizona, it was as though he stood "face to face with myself in a mirror." Shedding his hippie trappings, he came to Los Angeles, moved in with the Unified Family and persuaded his wife and their two children to join him. That was two years ago and he has never regretted a moment of it.

There was a young man who had been converted to the Divine Principle after dissatisfaction with his parental Baptist faith. While in the air force and stationed in various parts of the globe, he had met foreign members of the Unified Family. He taped his interviews and discussions with these scattered disciples of Sun Myung Moon, recorded their hymn-singing, and claimed that the Divine Principle movement was a first important breakthrough in the international life-style of an interfaith religion.

Another member, a Catholic girl, had found what she called new spiritual understanding and reality in the Divine Principle. So strong was her dedication to the Unified Family that her parents feared she was being held in the movement against her will. They came to Los Angeles from "back east" only to be convinced that their daughter had found a faith which, to her, was precious.

There was Jerry, who testified he had been a hippie at age thirteen. Throughout his high school years he had been engrossed in Plato and other philosophers, and was led to the Unified Family through a cousin who was a jazz musician. The change in his cousin's life had been so impressive that the musician had already converted both his sister and his parents to the movement.

And there was a young chiropractor from New York who became Lee's special friend. He had studied esoteric religions, had taken the Rosicrucian course, and was interested in various metaphysical movements, but never until he found the Divine Principle had he felt in possession of the "total truth."

Lee wrote me saying, "Family members like to tell how the Holy Spirit led the chiropractor to a meeting one Sunday morning. He heard his first lecture in the afternoon and joined the Family that night. It is this cross section of vocations and faiths that impresses me very much. Members come from almost every part of the country. Some of the girls have been go-go dancers, singers, secretaries and college students. Several have been on drugs. All were searching for something to give them understanding and purpose in the midst of our pseudo, plastic world. The Divine Principle becomes their guide, and the atmosphere of Love and Truth within the Family constitutes their purpose. Red, yellow, black, white are no longer just idealistic Sunday-school stuff, but God's one great family of all mankind.

Not only does Jesus love this colorful group, I do, too, and I've decided to join them."

3

So he moved in with the Unified Family, into a big house where, because of the need for space, everyone slept in sleeping bags. If this seemed uncomfortable and lacking in utopian style, it was, at least, a good way of paying "indemnity." Indemnity may have been used a bit facetiously in connection with sleeping on the floor instead of comfortably in bed, but the message was clear. Satan, according to Divine Principle teachings, tries his satanic best to divert and discourage those who follow the Divine Principle way. He puts inconveniences in the paths of aspiring members. He makes things tough. This is the devil's pernicious way of making you pay for what you learn from God.

Hence, *indemnity*. It is "protection or exemption from loss or damage, past or to come." Indemnity means that God never forgives man unconditionally for his shortcomings because this would be contrary to Divine Principle. It is not enough for a person simply to desire or intend to return to God's presence after having lived in the world (Satan's domain). Like the prodigal son, a man must make his way step by step from the husks of life back to his Father's house. Only when, by his own volition, is he within sight of that heavenly house, will his Father come forth to meet him.

"The Law of Indemnity is like bankruptcy," say the teachings. "Imagine that you owe someone $1,000, but all you can scrape together is $50. Your creditor accepts what you have and forgives the balance. This is what God does. Satan, however, is not as generous as God. He will not forgive anything. He demands 100 percent payment, and, if it is not paid willingly, he will exact it in the form of illness, pain, worry, fear, doubt, inconveniences, moods, depression, and many other diverse and subtle methods. There is, however, a way in which these debts can be paid off quickly. Conscious payment of physical indemnity or restitution in everything we do removes Satan's opportunity to attack us. God will not let Satan claim more than his due."

Therefore, self-disciplinary action such as fasting, or cheerfully washing dishes, mopping floors, cooking, or even sleeping in sleeping bags is a way of putting it over on Satan and magnifying the Lord.

The Unified Family, according to Lee at this phase of his odyssey, was doing exactly that, in the secret recognition that the Lord had already come. They were one great, happy fellowship unified in love, with each person sharing the various household responsibilities. Room and board were free for the first two weeks. Then, if one decided to stay, the weekly rate was pegged at $25. Many of the members of the Los Angeles Family attended college while others had jobs and went to night school. The Family ate together, worked and shared together, with men and women segregated only in their sleeping quarters. As far as sex was concerned, Lee insisted that morals could hardly have been higher or attitudes more spiritualized.

This was understandable for, according to the *Divine Principle*, the "blessing of marriage" seemed far and away the most important and extraordinary of all the teachings. For while the *Divine Principle* covered a wide range of topics all the way from "the Principle of Creation" to "the Principle of the New Age," the relationship of marriage and salvation was most graphic and, for me at least, if not for Lee, the most unclear.

For example, in order to receive Mr. Moon's marriage blessing it was necessary, according to Divine Principle requirements, to be either "a pure virgin or bachelor." This was the first consideration and was regarded as purely reasonable and elementary. Since we are all fallen human beings, we must by virtue of Sun Moon's edict, be restored "reversely." That is, we must have children first, before marriage. By this is meant *spiritual* children.

The Divine Principle plan is for each bachelor or virgin to lead at least three persons to the state of consciousness where they, too, can be blessed in marriage. These six (three spiritual children brought by the bachelor and three by the virgin) together with the bachelor and virgin constitute a family of eight, and eight, according to Sun Moon's theory, represents the eight members of "Adam's and Noah's families." The symbol here is that "as Noah's family restored the world to God, so modern man must restore and redeem his satanic domain." He must be fruitful and multiply, but the phrase refers first to spiritual children and then to physical offspring.

"Since married life in the satanic world is not recognized by God," said Sun Moon in a lecture titled "On Blessing and Witnessing," "the husband and wife must go their own ways as brother and sister. God has been working for six thousand years and now His providence is entering the seven thousandth year. According to the *Principle*, husband and wife must be separated for seven years. . . . Married couples must abstain from the marriage relationship at least seven months. There are those in Korea who have been abstaining for over seven years and live as sister and brother. Those whom God loves just can't continue their married life. God strikes their bodies and they can't continue.

"If the wife only follows the *Principle*, great conflict arises in the family. The same is true if only the husband follows. So our church has been accused of destroying families. This is not true. We are uniting them. Other churches blame us and accuse us, saying that the husbands or wives have found other mates in our church. This is not true. In other words, your leader and the people in Korea have made indemnity for you, so you are required to abstain only seven months instead of seven years. We are the only group who does such a thing. On this matter, there is no generosity. It must be done this way. If couples don't do this, their blessing will be postponed. After you are blessed again, your marriage will be eternal."

It was not easy going and not always clear just what was symbol and what was law. Nor was Sun Myung Moon much help when he said that he himself had not married until his fortieth year.

"Before my marriage in 1960," he once said, "the married couples in our church abstained for several years. If I wasn't married, how could they be married? But after my marriage, I shortened the time. Now you can abstain seven months before you receive your blessing. That means that before your blessing, a husband and wife should remain as bachelor and virgin for at least seven months and come before me as brother and sister. Then they can be blessed in marriage."

To Lee, despite the unorthodox regulations and the complicated interpretation on blessing and marriage and spiritual children and restoration through abstinence, whether for seven years or seven months, the Unified Family was high adventure. It was committed to a cause and it demonstrated spiritual togetherness. Every day began with family devotions. Evenings were filled with lectures, study, and singing. And then there was also witnessing.

Witnessing aroused Lee's first critical concern. He went with members of the Unified Family to such obviously productive spots as Griffith Park, Hollywood Boulevard, UCLA, and the Aquarius Theatre. Armed with literature which had a psychedelic flair and was heavy on the pitch for love and peace, he mingled with the crowds and gave away the Divine Principle handouts. The mastheads said:

OVERCOME WITH TENSION?
CONFUSION? INDECISION? DOUBT? WORRY?
MOVE UP!
BREAK AWAY!
HERE'S YOUR WAY TO LIFE, LOVE AND
HAPPINESS!
JOIN A CONSTRUCTIVE NON-VIOLENT
REVOLUTION!

These broadsides brought people to the lecture sessions and often netted new members, but what bothered Lee was that the Divine Principle movement promised more than it could fulfill. It spoke about the cosmic vision of Sun Myung Moon and of revolutionary new relationships between God and man, and man and his environment, as if the Divine Principle system had already proved them all out. It held out tantalizing offers of "a powerful new understanding underlying physical sciences, social sciences, history, philosophy and religion as if it already had the endorsement of specialists in these fields. It assured its followers that it had new insights into psychic phenomena, ESP, and other "phenomenal evidence cited as to the beginning of the New Age." Witnessing made Lee feel different from the rest of the world and suggested an apartness of the kind he had sought to escape from in Pentecostalism. It was togetherness he wanted.

Occasionally he went with other members of the Family to spiritualistic meetings to see what was going on, and, if possible, to corroborate some of the testimony that had allegedly come through Arthur Ford about the power and meaning of the Divine Principle movement.

Practically every member of the Family claimed some kind of mediumistic manifestation, either in the form of dreams and visions, or materializations and communications with spirit entities. Family members did not want it publicized that they were actually seeking psychic manifestations, because mediums were not necessarily considered spiritually advanced just because they could demonstrate supernormal phenomena. After all, they were merely receiving stations, and it would be necessary to prove to the spirits whether or not they were of God. Yet clairvoyance, clairaudience, and automatic writing were highly regarded, especially by the Korean groups. All of which increased Lee's doubts about the actual differences between the Unified Family and any other spiritually-oriented fellowships elsewhere in other denominations.

Perhaps there was less difference between them than he had imagined unless, of course, it could be proved that the New Messiah had already come and lived among them in the person of Sun Myung Moon.

4

It was exciting news to the members of the Unified Family to learn that Mr. Moon was returning to the United States from Korea. He was to be accompanied by his wife, an interpreter, and several presidents of the movement in Korea, Japan, and the Americas.

Everyone in the Family was ecstatic at the announcement. The house was thoroughly cleaned inside and out, prayers were spoken, and the study material was reviewed, especially those portions relating to the "Lord of the Second Advent." While there were no textual sources that clearly stated, "Sun Myung Moon is the promised Messiah," there were sufficient inferences to persuade even the newest members that a world avatar would soon be in their midst. Biblical prophecies about Christ's return were discussed in the lecture periods, and excerpts from Miss Kim's *Divine Principle* were liberally cited.

In writing about the geographical location from which the new Messiah would emerge, Miss Kim explained, "It is apparent that the chosen nation for the final dispensation must be one where Christianity is strong and where the major Oriental religions are deeply rooted. To be chosen as the universal altar, this nation must itself be divided into two sections symbolizing Cain and Abel. In this way the nation represents the world, which is also divided into two blocs. To fulfill its mission as the chosen nation, this country must be united—Abel must subjugate Cain on this land. 'The strangest war ever fought by man, that war in Korea,' has providential significance. The Koreans and sixteen nations of the United Nations, representing justice, fought in the war and shed blood, which will serve as a condition of indemnity for the establishment of the Father's kingdom."

There was another bit of circumstantial evidence being noised about. When new members of the Unified Family asked, "How will we recognize the One that is to come?" the answer was, "You will know him through his revelations. Watch and see. Jesus is even now manifesting himself and directing people to his successor."

This reference pointed in large part to a pamphlet, *Revelation for the New Age,* written by the English mystic Anthony Brooke. His treatise described the worldwide activities of a spiritual entity who materialized and gave instructions concerning the New Age. The entity called himself "Truth," and was believed by members of the Unified Family to be the psychic projection of Mr. Moon.

So the entourage came. The cars drew up with their religious celebrities, and with songs and greetings the delegation was ushered into the large room for the in-

formal get-together. Lee, who arrived late, had an em-
barrassing moment. He could not distinguish the
"Promised One" from the other Koreans. They were
all pleasant, gracious, and seemingly radiant, and it was
not until the solidly built, sober-eyed sage was pointed
out to him that Lee knew who he was. Why, Lee
wondered, was the recognition not more intuitive and
convincing?

Then the members of the Los Angeles Family enter-
tained their guests with songs, piano and guitar solos
and dances, and Mr. Moon returned the favor with
a solo of his own, as did other members of his group.
Throughout the festivities, he was extremely quiet and
unpretentious, doing nothing to draw attention to himself while modestly accepting the inevitable attention
that was directed his way. Later, when he prayed, it
was an intimate person-to-person talk with God, as if
the Lord were a faithful friend of long standing. There
was no pleading or agonizing or struggle in his voice, no
begging in his words. It was a prayer of adoration, and
a few tears glistened on his brown cheeks when he had
finished.

Lee was impressed and thoughtful. By what credentials was this man truly the incarnated Christ or even
the universal avatar whose image was being developed
more and more by the ardor of his devotees? How was
he different? What were the telltale signs? How was a
person to know and what could a person believe? He
listened engrossed to Mr. Moon's lectures on the following evening. His speech reminded him of the dialect
he had often heard in Pentecostalism when people
spoke in tongues. He took note of many of the quota-

tions which the interpreter stressed as being of special significance:

We are a wild olive tree. To become part of the true olive tree we must cut off our carnal mind and be grafted into the mind of Christ. By engrafting ourselves with Christ, we become Sons of God.

If Adam had not fallen, God could not have dwelt in him. Adam is the substantial body of God, the Spirit, God in flesh.

Man and woman together are from God. Eve would then have been the wife of God. Adam and Eve's love should have been God-centered with God in the middle. Because Satan beguiled Eve, love has become satanic. We are born of satanic parents because our lineage comes from the first Adam who fell.

You enter heaven only in couples. When you meet your ideal mate it is as though you have searched through 7000 years of dark history.

Satan's final strategy is to stimulate young people to Adam and Eve's sin of adultery.

There were question periods and young people who had come to inquire rather than to pray were unhesitant to get at what they called the nitty-gritty of the Divine Principle program.

"What makes Mr. Moon think he is the Messiah?" was flung at the interpreter.

"Study the *Divine Principle* and you will know," came the answer.

"Was there some specific point in your life when you realized you were the one whom God had been seeking to fulfill the restoration?"

Sun Moon replied, "From childhood I was clairvoyant and clairaudient. I could see through people, see their spirits. I had a very strong desire to live a life of high dimension. When I was twelve I started praying for extraordinary things. I asked for wisdom greater than Solomon's, faith greater than the apostle Paul's and for love greater than the love Jesus had. This is not a usual thing for one twelve years old. When I was sixteen I knew definitely what my mission was to be."

He spoke of his "thousands of followers in Korea" and of "over one thousand in Japan." He said, "Even the Japanese government is interested in our movement because of these young people's sincerity and philosophy. Many influential people are interested in our movement and some are already members. During my two weeks' stay in Japan, five leading members of Buddhism and Shintoism joined our group through the guidance and messages of the spirit world. In Korea we have several Buddhist friends. They also witness that our movement will unify all religions. Buddha comes to them and says that his mission is now over and that his followers should go to Mr. Moon because he is the one to unify all religions 'like rivers run into the ocean.' Confucius says the same thing in a different expression. He also tells his followers to go to our movement, that his own mission is over."

So Sun Myung Moon came and went and the Unified Family continued its collectivistic living, its witnessing and its silent affirming that the Lord of the Second Advent dwelt in their midst. But as far as Lee was concerned, the cause was losing a great deal of its impact. The generalities, the promises, the purported testimony of the spirit world, the queer twists of scripture and the obvious attempt to fit Mr. Moon into the new age rather than to find him responsible for the formation of the age itself were factors which divided Lee's loyalties and increased his concern.

Most of all, he felt that for him, at least, spiritual evidence had to be self-confirming. Something within him had to substantiate the teachings, some inner spark needed to enforce the claim that the Paraclete had indeed risen out of South Korea and that the Word had once more been made flesh in the stocky figure of Sun Myung Moon. These assurances were still wanting, and all the endorsement of psychics and mediums could not persuade him of their truth.

So he said "Good-bye" to the Unified Family, gave his honest blessings to the Divine Principle movement, and took his leave to continue his odyssey, taking with him the inspiration and the ideal of young people who, in their longing for answers and togetherness, still firmly felt that they had found a faith.

Some nine months later Lee earnestly confided to me that the objectives of the Unified Family still tantalized him and that, even now, when he dropped in on religious services at Unity centers or worshiped in Pentecostal assemblies, a song ran through his mind:

> Gonna build a kingdom on this sad old ground;
> Gonna build a kingdom all around!
> Gonna call it heaven 'cause that's what it'll be,
> A place of beauty, peace and joy for you and me!

I got in touch with Lee again when a letter came from the Washington headquarters of the movement. In gentle terms, the president of HSA-UWC (Holy Spirit Association for the Unification of World Christianity)

wrote me saying, "There are now Divine Principle training centers in 25 major cities of the United States, as
well as in about 20 countries. This October (1970) in
Seoul, 700 couples from seven nations will be wed
simultaneously by Sun Myung Moon. Five couples
from the United States will participate. We feel the
wedding of the 700 couples represents an international
foundation for a unified family of mankind."

Would Lee have believed that this could happen—
seven hundred marriages en masse in keeping with
bachelor-virgin regulations of the *Divine Principle?*

"I think so," he said, "for there are many like me in
the world, searching, wishing, listening, and wondering, too, about the day—and the way—in which Jesus
will come again."

7
The Jesus People

1

The Jesus People!

What they did with "Rock of Ages" and "Lead Kindly Light"! How they lifted "The Old Rugged Cross" and "Were You There When They Crucified My Lord"! How they pulled out the stops on "Saved By Grace" and stoned us with the scream of souped-up guitars in their medleys of Pentecostal hymns!

What have *we* ever done with "Rock of Ages" or "Lead Kindly Light" but lull ourselves to Sunday morning sleep? Where has the gospel of good news gotten us except in and out of a sombre Sabbath service?

The Jesus People are of another breed. Another generation. Another age bracket, say 15 to 25. Another background. Many of them have been on drugs, or better said, have come off drugs. A great number have emerged from the underground. They include college students, college graduates, college drop-outs, high school drop-outs, church drop-outs, hippies. Some have been sex perverts. Others have been as Simon pure as members of the church establishment consider themselves to be. All of them, however, believe they have been called and touched and changed and powered by the Holy Spirit.

If you are over 30, you may have difficulty understanding the depth of their passion. If you are over 40, you will find yourself saying, "But when I was their age. . . ." If you have passed the half-century mark, their high-voltage music and their testimonies shrieked over their high-gain microphones will make you wish for cotton in your ears. No matter. They are targeting their message at their generation, not yours, and when they get to be 30, 40, or 50—that's another story. They are what they are and where they are *now*. As far as they are concerned, this is their day and now is the accepted time of their salvation.

As I meet them and observe their phenomenon, it often strikes me that members of one's own family can seem stranger than strangers from foreign lands.

For me to say this is strangest of all, for I, too, had the baptism of—or in—the Holy Spirit when I was in my hippie years. So graphic and life-changing was my "upper-room" encounter that I made my confession in a recent book *(The Inner Ecstasy),* and bared my believing heart to the calculated skepticism of those to whom glossolalia is sheer gibberish and who know the Paraclete only as a silent partner in the Holy Trinity.

More than that, even those who claimed—along

157

with Timothy Leary—a mystical experience through the use of LSD were no wierdos to me. I tried mescaline for the sake of research and have many adult friends among the hallucinogenic experimenters.

Even my exposure to the non-Christian Hare Krishna boys was not beyond the reach of an inner affinity, and yoga and Vedanta are precious to me. But what seemed strange was the fact that historic Christianity, with its 157 contemporary denominations, its 200,000 American churches, its nearly one billion members around the world, could not fulfill the quest of our acid-headed youth, whose search was as sincere as mine had been when I was reveling in their brave young years.

The difference between this batch of young revolutionaries and me was that, when it came to religion, they were no longer even window-shopping on Church Street. The flamboyant church pages which had me ogle-eyed with claims of miracles, evangelistic commercials, and tantalizing titles aimed straight at my anxious heart left these liberated young people absolutely cold as they freely and fearlessly trudged across the country and around the world. They turned away from the family pew as arrogantly as they did from barber chairs. They were not about to be herded or coerced into panic no matter which professional ecclesiastic sounded the alarm. They were, in fact, anti-church, anti-theology, and, if you came right down to it, anti-Christianity, as we once knew it, we who at their age used to march solemnly to catechetical instruction and obediently repeat our "I believe. . . ."

I am talking about the young people of the hip-culture, whether long-haired or short, and of the denominational defectors, whether dirty or clean. I am talking about your son and daughter, who would rather listen to rock music or read the *Book of the Dead* than go with you to the Sunday service, and who now would best of all go where the action is in a Holy Spirit revival straight off the street, drawn by changed lives, speaking in tongues, and the charismatic wonder of converted lives.

The Jesus People.

2

For the sake of orientation in the social scene, let me say just a word about the Krishna Consciousness movement since it was mentioned above. If you have been in any of our large cities in the United States and Canada, the incessant chant may still be ringing in your ears:

> Hare Krishna, Hare Krishna,
> Krishna, Krishna, Hare Hare!
> Hare Rama, Hare Rama,
> Rama, Rama, Hare Hare!

If you listened long enough you also heard Buddha and Jesus praised and blessed, though it is Krishna who, in a special way, is "God."

We are talking now not about the Jesus People, but about part of the phenomenon, the fact that young Americans, intelligent, perceptive, and of the kind that used to make up Protestant and Catholic youth work, will shave their heads, paint their faces, don the saffron robe and chant and dance barefooted in the streets, lost in ecstatic absorption and seeming for all the world to be reincarnations of the *sankirtana,* the chanting parties that roamed the Indian roads a thousand years ago. And not young men only, girls as well, college-trained and college-bred, wrapped in saris and lost in bliss.

I have listened to the chants and the beating of the bongo drums and watched the whirling Krishna dervishes until they have haunted me in my sleep. I have sat in their love feasts and visited their ashrams and tried to understand their contention that Hare Krishna sets your universe in order and that the *Bhagavad-Gita* is the only book you need to make your world go round.

The wild joy, the transcendental wonder, the jubilation and the passion—higher than sex and fiercer than bodily desire—are not faked. Krishna to them is the King of Moons, the lotus flower, the everlasting avatar sending his messengers to turn on the spiritual power.

My wonder, when I saw the hypnotic figures dancing in front of the big name stores: Marshall Field's in Chicago, Macy's in New York, Hudson's Bay in Vancouver, Bullock's in Los Angeles, on traffic-jammed corners in Montreal, Seattle, Philadelphia, wherever I have heard them and spoken with their group leaders, my wonder has to do with the question that will come up again with the Jesus People, how do you inspire masses of young America to follow a faith? Where do you find, as is the case among the Krishna devotees, young people cut out of the same stock, so much so that they look alike, speak alike, think alike, as if they had been spun off an assembly line, yet call themselves free and saved and glorified?—and I ask myself whether the church-at-large ever thinks about this or cares about it or wonders about it at all?

Here is Krishna Consciousness, a non-Christian movement, nonsectarian they call it, less than five years old, with the surreptitious title, BACK TO GODHEAD and with headquarters in twenty-four North American cities. A floating generation, which would not be bothered by names as far out as Zephaniah, Zechariah, or Malachi, speaks fluently of their guru-organizer, A. C. Bhaktivedanta Swami, makes their pilgrimage to New Vrindabahn in Moundsville, West Virginia, quotes from the Vedas, calls their leader Prabhupada, and dwells on the Ksirodakasayi Vishnu, the Paramatma or Supersoul.

Instead of Jesus, Krishna. Instead of the Bible, the *Bhagavad-Gita*. Instead of the Beatitudes, the Eightfold Path. Instead of the challenge to overcome sin, the injunction to overcome rebirth, disease, old age, and death. Instead of chuches, the streets. Instead of silent prayers, chanting in the business districts.

Bhaktivedanta Swami tells it as it is, or at least, as he sees it to be,

"This chanting is the process of clearing the dust accumulated on the heart. Our relationship with God is eternal. It cannot be broken. But because of *maya* (illusion) we are tempted to forget him. If we chant this Holy Name of God, Hare Krishna, then *maya* will not act, and we shall very quickly understand our relationship with God. That is the process. Krishna Consciousness is not a bogus movement. It is scientific, authorized. Any scientist, any logician may come, and we shall prove that there is God and that we have an eternal relationship with him. So if you want happiness, then you must take to this Krishna Consciousness movement. Otherwise the human race is doomed."

When a reporter reminded him that, "Mr. Billy Graham makes people God-conscious in a different way. What do you think of him?" Bhaktivedanta Swami replied, "I do not what is Billy Graham (sic), I follow the *Bhagavad-Gita* as it is. Krishna says you give up all nonsense occupations and simply surrender to him, and he will take charge of you and give you protection. This is our philosophy."

3

And now the Jesus People. You will understand them only in the context of their generation: acid, pot, grass, rock festivals, campus violence, educational revolt, Vietnam, the draft, the government, the police, the radicals, the sexual revolution, and an impassioned quest for meaning and a place in life, a generation with its own news media, its own philosophy, its own language.

And we must see it in the context of our generation which, viewed across the credibility and communication gaps, appears to them to be pseudo-religious, culturally faked, economically frustrated; a pharmaceutically drug-crazed generation; a sex-crazed generation where birth control is opposed by a celibate priesthood, abortion laws are made the subject of ecclesiastical debates; a generation passing on to them a world dying in its environmental poison, sociologically and spiritually blocked by its moment of truth.

"What we are doing," a member of the Jesus People told me, "is living Christ the way the Christian church once said he should be lived, but didn't live him for two thousand years. It did everything *but* live him. It made statues of him and built buildings for him and made money off of him, but it never lived him or loved him, and that is what we plan to do. We went to our churches and couldn't find him. We went to our parents and couldn't find him. We went to college and couldn't find him, but we found him in our own way through the power of the Holy Spirit."

The Jesus People. At this writing no one knows how many there are, or exactly where they are, or whether they will ever be consolidated. But I have a hunch that they are the avant garde of a new image of Christian life and the seed of a new church which may be as different from the church we know as the 747 is from the first flyable plane.

It would be safer and less prophetic to say that their Holy-Ghost-inspired fervor is a passing phase, a first love, something many of us went through in our own overlapping years. We could say that they will get this out of their systems and settle down and soon be elders and vestrymen and deacons in the churches of the establishment, but for the fact that they are a new breed. If they ever return to the church, they will change the churches before the churches can presume to alter them.

That, at least, was how it seemed to me the night I sat in Pender Auditorium in Vancouver, B.C., and heard the spokesmen for the "Jesus Army" tell it the way it seemed to them.

"Attention, troops!" shouted leader Jim Palosaari, standing on stage with strong hands wrapped around the platform microphone, "To the streets! I know it's raining out there, but march out and bring them in! There must be three or four hundred roaming the night and waiting to be called!"

There were three or four hundred of us already assembled in the aging hall where we were waiting for the meeting to begin, but at Jim's authoritative command, some thirty long-haired male volunteers and a dozen equally long haired girls rose from their chairs and made for the doors.

"I don't know what the program will be like," Jim continued hugging up to the microphone, "but, thank God, we don't have to follow a routine. All we have to do is follow Jesus. Let's have a handclap for Jesus!"

We had one and the young musicians came in with their guitars and took their places at the xylophone and piano, and we were off on an invocation of song which put the message into our hearts and voices, "I'm Born Again an' Never Goin' to Die!"

The sound was turned up to a deafening pitch. The few recruits of oldsters sprinkled through the hip-culture congregation were conspicuous by their cringing backs from the full impact of the blasting sounds, but they could not refrain from clapping, not only for Jesus but for the sake of a rhythm that got into their blood as the beat went on, and as the young people began to herd in others like themselves whom they found some-where on the rain-soaked avenues and persuaded them that an invading army had come to town, come up from Seattle and Portland and Spokane to convert the hard core of Vancouver's vagrants who had missed Jesus somewhere along the way. Gradually the balcony was filled, and the auditorium was crowded and The Vision, a rock band of converted Jesus People, was giving out with original songs that rocked the ancient hall.

Recent publicity had given an assist in attracting the growing audience. The story, and true, in fact, was that the "Army" had been held up at the border by Canadian immigration officials. When interrogated, the troopers admitted ("Jesus People never lie") that they had been on drugs at some point in their lives, that they had criminal records, that they had no permanent dwelling place at the moment. Some of them posted bond for themselves and others to get across what has always been considered one of the friendliest of international boundaries. Somehow they made it, as legally as possible, and as gallantly as if they had been escorted. Well, they had. Jesus, they said, was right there, walking in the lead, urging them on, granting them his grace, telling them that boundaries and borders are made by man, not God.

Earlier that day I had dropped around to visit the headquarters of the Jesus Army. A week ago it had been an abandoned house in the 1700 block on Seventh Avenue, little more than a shack, ready to be torn down. The realty company said it did not mind if the Army used it for a while. The tiny, dirty-white picket fence around the two story patched-up building was falling apart. The weeds were high, the steps rickety, the seven rooms barren with cracked and broken plaster walls and a few pieces of cast-off furniture. But there was space for sleeping bags and blankets and a stove that could be made to work, and there were several sagging shelves which held a worn copy of the Scriptures and Pentecostal magazines and stacks of yellow handbills with an overprint upon a psychedelic background that said:

JESUS PEOPLE'S ARMY—REVOLUTIONARY YOUTH MOVEMENT!

"It may not look like much around here," a young private in the Army said impersonally, "but there wasn't much in Bethlehem, either. Right?"

And I got to thinking that the Twelve who followed him in Galilee may have looked as nondescript or fully as picturesque as those now on the Pender stage. The Luilson-McKinley Jesus People Band of Spokane was shaking the hall to its foundations. This crowded congregation would never have been allowed to get into a church like First Congregational of Los Angeles, for example. Worn and faded Levis, ankh crosses, mini skirts, maxi skirts, ponchos, sandals, boots, bare feet, beards, granny glasses—and near me a young fellow had slumped in his seat ever since the troops brought him in. Hands stuffed deep into his pants pockets, his eyes glassy, he sat there frozen, pillowing his head against his luxuriant mass of hair on the curved metal frame of his folding chair. Every once in a while he deigned to extract his hands, clap listlessly, smile, and then go back into his coma.

He came to life only when the star of the evening, Linda Meissner, publicized as "straight from the pages

of *The Cross and the Switchblade,*" embraced the
microphone and began to testify. She started on a
pitch of such intensity that I told myself it could not
be sustained for more than five minutes at the most.
After nearly half an hour she was still going strong and
growing, if anything, in passion and power. Earlier
someone had said that Spurgeon once said, "The reason
I have such attention is because I set myself on fire and
people come to see me burn." This applied to Linda.

"Listen to us!" she resounded. "You don't have to
like us or love us or help us, but listen to us! We went
to the hip-communes because we want love! We can't
stand hatred, we have awakened, we have walked out
of the churches, we have walked out of society, we
have walked out of our homes, we are walking with
Jesus! Listen to us! Something is happening! Something
is happening in the world! Do you see it? Can you hear
it? Peace is no longer a word, a symbol! Peace is something real! We hate Christianity as it is, we hate religion, we hate the church! We love a PERSON! Listen
to us! You hear? We love a PERSON! We love JESUS
CHRIST! We intend to reach our goal through a MAN!"

Something moved next to me, shaking me out of the
trance that Linda Meissner had instilled. Someone was
on his feet. My sallow-faced, luxuriantly-haired recruit
was standing with fluttering eyes uplifted and implor-
ing arms outstretched to heaven, and the only reason
no one paid attention to him was because he was one
of the many who had assumed the same statuesque
position and were impatiently anticipating the coming
of the MAN.

According to my interviews with members of the

Army, young people are excitedly seeking and finding him all across the land.

"We are called THE SPIRIT in Spokane, THE WORD in Yakima, and AGAPE in Seattle," said the editor of the *Jesus People's Paper,* "but we're all members of the same body, that of Jesus Christ. He is starting to put us together."

He indicated that the major movements were located up and down the west coast and radiating out from various cities along the coastline route. Underground newspapers were helping in the consolidation, carrying announcements of meetings, and reporting on activities. The controversial *Hollywood Free Press* was offering bumper stickers: JESUS PEOPLE UNITE! GIVE JESUS A CHANCE! JESUS IS MY BAG! I'M HIGH ON THE LOVE OF MY JESUS!

Agape, a Seattle publication, offered a list of 125 Christian communes or "houses" which have sprung up in the American West and Southwest, to serve as both retreat centers and revival pockets where the prodigals can find a peaceful place to pause long enough for the MAN to lay his hand on them.

4

One of these revival pockets of particular power is located on Crescent Heights Boulevard in Hollywood, California. Operating under the Christian Foundation, it has become a nerve center for both the expansion and the consolidation of a movement similar to the Jesus People's Army. Under the dynamic leadership of Sue and Tony Alamo, the bungalow-style house close to the

Sunset Strip has become the mecca for young people of all races and creeds who have turned off drugs and become newly turned on by Christ. Reborn, they are crusading with a vengeance against sin, drugs, Satan, and against young people's reluctance to "try Jesus" as they have tried and found him,

My introduction to this intensive redemptive process left me in a quandary. For one thing, on my first visit I arrived at the crowded chapel room just as the singing had started. The place was jammed, as it was on future visits and as it is on every night, but, as is also the custom, a young convert will usually offer you his or her place and make you feel immediately at home.

I felt even closer than that. The spirited singing took me back to my Pentecostal days with the Assembly of God people, only there was more fire here than we ever kindled in our most inspired hymn-sings. The Holy Spirit was definitely in evidence and the rapture was flowing. I accepted the proffered chair which the bearded youth vacated for me, but there was no thought of sitting down. Everyone was standing, singing, swaying, laughing, or weeping with joy as if the good news of the gospel had finally come to stay. Steel guitars plugged into light sockets on the cramped and crowded stage, swinging tambourines, the shriek of a flute, the twang of the piano, everything was in perfect synchonism with Spirit. The performance was loud (I could understand why the neighbors frequently complained to the police that the "hippie church" was disturbing the peace). It was wondrous (I could see why nostalgic senior citizens often dropped around). It was convincing (I realized there was not only life left in the old songs but also power in the blood).

After some twenty enchanted minutes of glory songs, interspersed with "hallelujahs" and "praise Jesus" there was a spontaneous moment of quiet reflection, deep and sincere. It was as silent as if the Lord had a special private message for each of us and wanted us to hear it by way of his still, small voice. It was precious, and what it said to me was, "Here is the answer to the spiritual need and challenge of our time. This questing generation which has run gamut from revolt to redemption is here as living proof that the answer is Jesus Christ. It has not only found the MAN but has caught the Spirit. This must be the new religion of a new age."

The truth is, as I sat there I began to formulate in my mind how I might help this cause by whatever resources were at my command. I was sold on the whole affair, and it had been a long time since anything had gotten hold of me with the conviction and empathy of these seemingly uncontrived moments of spiritual reality.

Then came the testimonials, the witnessing. Minute-long or minute-short confessions were given in rapid-fire order by some seventy-five young people who sprang to the lectern microphone to tell how the Lord had saved their souls. Their voices were sharp, clipped, and accusing. They were warning the sinners that a yawning gulf stretched between them and the saving grace of the Christ, that time was short, that God was impatient, and that heaven or hell was waiting.

Typical statements, "You better get right with God

or you'll burn. . . . You may never live to see the morning unless you get right with Jesus. . . . There's only one way to get with it, get with him or be damned to hell. . . . This could be your last chance. . . . Repent or perish. . . . My parents are pleading with me to come home. Hell no, I won't go. I'm with Jesus!"

The longer I listened, the more the feeling of fraternity that had thrilled me faded away. Bit by bit the wonder and joy of the singing, the radiant faces, the kids you thought you'd like to embrace and bless became a different kind of Jesus Army, a highly exclusive, far-right army ready to condemn and sentence those whose sensitivity might still see Jesus as the Lord of love.

Of course, the argument was that the greatest love of all is for Jesus to snatch an erring soul out of the devil's hands and that this requires force and even fear. That was the point explained to me by Sue and Tony Alamo. They contended that you do not persuade youngsters to kick the drug habit or crawl out of the pits of sin by simply reminding them that "Jesus loves you." They do not believe it works this easily, and I suppose they must follow the guidance of their years of experience and the prompting of their inner voice. There are traditional churches, however, notably Hollywood Presbyterian, which have had astonishing success with a softer approach to the citizens of the hip-culture.

Nonetheless, the Jesus People of the Christian Foundation are moving forward, doubling their membership every three or four months, building communes, working untiringly among the "street people," testifying, sacrificing, witnessing, stirring up the Christian con-

171

science, getting decisions for Christ, and stressing the apocalyptic evidence of the "End Time" of our age. Ministers and businessmen have become interested in the Foundation's process of spiritual rehabilitation, and the advocates of fundamental Christianity are generally on their side. Assistance comes not only in the form of moral support and prayer but in contributions of money, commodities, and supplies. Several ministers serve as "diggers," that is, co-workers who collect foodstuff from bakeries, supermarkets, and the like and deliver them for free to the commune commissaries.

Here again, when we realize the dependence of this oncoming generation on the establishment which they so consistently condemn, we wonder whether they will not eventually take their places in society and play the same role that most of us assume after our "over-thirty" years. It could be that the principles that govern our lives will some day govern theirs: the need for material substance, family obligations, social concerns, the imprint of the collective unconscious, and the stark fact that our age is dealing with problems, sociological and psychological, for which there were no actual parallelisms in Jesus' time.

But, for now, though we who are older may presume to tell the story, the Jesus People who are standing at our door can tell it best.

"We have studied the philosophers," one convert wrote in the *Jesus People's Paper,* "from Lenin to Marx, and the surrealists like Nitche (sic) and Dostoyevsky, and materialists like Gurdjieff and Rand, through the drop-outs Camus and Miller, and the searchers like Hesse and Hemingway, or a Huxlean (sic) exploration of a bravely dying world. We dutifully followed our national heroes—Karoac (sic), who led us on the road, Ginsberg, who crooned to us, and Kilbran (sic), who whispered that we were really getting somewhere. With the Beatles blissfully humming in the background, we became strangers in a strange new land with Timothy Leary, Inc., with whom we dropped out to tune in on a world where everyone is perpetually turned on.

"We followed every new program with bleats of joy into a never-never land where American Indian legends and eastern occultism met together in one huge Hiroshima. It was very nice up there on top of the mushroom, but what about when you have to crash?

"Then there was this PERSON who saw us standing around with nothing to do, wondering what was going on, and He said, 'Would you like to have something to occupy your head and soul the rest of your life? Follow me!'

"Well, He was so beautiful, and He wasn't on a big ego trip like the other gurus we had tried, and He had the heaviest message we ever heard any leader rap, in the simple language of the people, and He promised us His personal backing to get the job done.

"He said, 'I've been watching you, and I like your kind of persistence. I've been looking for laborers who will tell it like it is. In return, I'll give you the reality you've been looking for all your life, not only up to the minute your body dies, but continuing on for all of eternity!'

"Then He told us that the first benefit that came with the plan was that He would personally clean us up from all the muck we had accumulated over the years, so that when we went out with His message, we'd shine with it. He scrubbed deep down, and it hurt, but when He finished, we felt fresh as the soft velvet sheen of a rose petal touched with dew or wind-blown wild alfalfa on a warm day. That MAN called JESUS had blown the scope of our minds till we could see where things were really at. He's gathering the people together and we'll stick with Him all the way, because He's been 100 percent perfect since we've known Him, and that's what we were looking for all along."

Maybe it was.

Still we wonder whether we didn't have what they were seeking all along, and whether, in our way, we found him, too, according to the manner of our questing in our time?

And will another generation, already hard on their heels, represent to them another breed of strangers rapping at *their* door?

8
Meeting the Challenge

1

When conclusions are beyond the range of logic, it should be permissible to resort to imagery, which is how I feel about commenting with any finality on the Strangers at the Door. There is something beyond the rational mind which must reveal itself in symbolism, for at this deeper level the authority is of the heart and spirit and touches something quite transpersonal.

At any rate, I am looking for a justification to take refuge for the moment in a rhetorical allusion to—walls!

I have always had an aversion to walls. Also a fascination for them. It all depends, as the poet said, on what we are walling in or walling out. "Something there is that doesn't love a wall, and wants it down."

What is that something? Love, perhaps. Love wants it down. But there is also something that admires a wall. Love, no doubt, when it remembers the devotion with which the wall was built and how the stones were selected and fitted together and how the builder paused to reflect upon his work.

Often in faraway, half-forgotten places, I have paused to touch old walls, walls still standing firm or crumbling, walls with overhanging vegetation, farm walls, city walls, castle walls, church walls. I love walls as long as they have gates or stiles or some way of getting through or over them, if for no other reason than to assert one's freedom and to see what the other side of the wall is like. It is also interesting to discover how people, walled out from me, feel about me, I who had been walled out from them.

The analogy is by no means perfect, but the symbolism is clear: the church architecturally, doctrinally, historically is a wall. I discovered this when, as a young minister, I tried to merge two churches in a small midwestern town.

I learned something about walls and the devotion with which the literal and symbolic stones were put in place: the memorial window dedicated to a loved one, the church organ donated in memory of a faithful parishioner, the church bell—a gift from a zealous defender of denominational rights—even the labor that went into the new roof and into decorations in the church parlors were part of the *wall,* to say nothing about "truths we have always believed," or "things we hold to be God-given," or commitments that must be obeyed because "they are the only way to salvation."

Now that I am in the fortunate position of religious researcher, rather than in the parish ministry, it is easy for me to say that if I had a church I would make it a

church of the Spirit, the Spirit of love, peace and compassion; a church *without* walls, without concern for
growth in membership or denominational prestige. I
would make clear my belief that the spirit of God is the
spirit of life, moving in and through all living things,
and whenever strangers came along, I would try to remember Gamaliel.

Heaven only knows how my concept would work
out in actual practice, but I have a hunch I would say
to everyone, "This is God's house. If you love God or
seek God, if you have a feeling for God or a longing
for God, if you have love to give or love to find, if you
have faith to share or the faith to look for faith, this is
your house, because it is the House of God."

I would leave my church perpetually open in the
belief that God's angels would protect the place. If
they didn't, I would put nothing in it that could be
vandalized or destroyed, and God would probably have
more room in which his presence could move about
more freely anyway.

I would send out the word through the consciousness
of prayer, inviting everyone of every faith to come and
bring the *darshan* (spiritual vibrations) of his presence
and leave some of it as a love offering to others who
might be seeking what another has already found.

I would begin my service by saying, "Now we will
sit in the silence, which is the universal language, and
feel the universal longing of the people of the world of
whom we are a part, and if we listen deeply enough and
long enough, chances are we will hear the still small
voice that everyman has heard, no matter when or

where he lived, when it was whispered to him that the life in him is the life of God personified."

Worshiping in my make-believe church with my make-believe congregation, I can imagine that my heart would often overflow with the joy and thrill of a strange mystique: the realization that men had sought and found God long before my parental faith began, and that they would be seeking and finding him long after my parental church is gone, which it almost is. And I would have to hold back tears of understanding as I let the concept of the Overchurch-of-the-Spirit clasp me in its arms, assuring me that it always was and is and always will be the Overchurch, a church without walls, in which there is no true salvation for any man unless there is salvation for all.

2

What would I do with him who gave the Christian church its name, or whose name we appropriated? What would I do with the mighty Cornerstone of the ecclesiastical wall, the "Rock" about which we sing? That question is not only beyond me, it is already answered. He is being recognized as the Cosmic Christ, and not by Pierre Teilhard only, but by mankind generally in its need for salvation in the present life, no less than in the life-to-come.

Clearly, this discovery of his cosmic consciousness dawned on us after we ourselves had fashioned him in such a wide variety of images. We gave him many faces. We still do. According to the profile of choice, we saw him as a long-haired revolutionary, at home in the remnants of hippie communes, chanting his Beatitudes to the sound of a steel guitar and a tambourine. We pictured him as a sallow Judge at God's right hand, eyeing the scales of justice. We presented him as a Man of Sorrows, a compassionate Pilgrim weeping over the city. We said that he is the Light and Laughter, the Joy and Peace and Prosperity of the world, bearing the gospel of good news. He is, in every country, the artist's model for the new man made in the image of native culture. He is humanist and theist, pacifist and warrior, Catholic, Protestant, Christian, non-Christian, churchman, cultist, half-Jew-half-Gentile, lending himself, sharing himself, dissecting himself, loved, promoted, exploited, explored and feared, wearing the masks of a thousand faiths.

Whatever he is, he is the churches' one foundation and the hope of the world.

His oneness will be recognized only when he is seen wherever his consciousness shines through. If he cannot be totally captured or comprehended by one denomination, neither can he be confined to one religion however universal its appeal or whatever its name. For among other things that he is, he is Spirit, and among his many faces is the face of humanity, God's face, in color as well as in black-and-white. And among his revelations to the world is the truth of his being, his incarnation and reincarnation since time began.

What of our fears of yesterday's non-Christian movements, the threat of heterodoxical ideologies, the heretics who were killed, the holy wars that were fought, the challenges of other messiahs that were beaten down, where are they now? What do they mean?

What were we defending, when he was his own defense? Whom were we shielding when he welcomed each open encounter? How could we hide him from others when they had already found so much of him among themselves?

This present challenge is again a divine paradox. *He* is there if we will but see, and the strangers at our door know he is there if *we* but acknowledge his presence. There is no place where he is not, and there never was a time or a world in which he has not been.

There *is* something that doesn't love a wall and wants it down.

3

I have lived long enough to be an eyewitness to the transmutations of institutionalized Christianity ever since Catholicism and Protestantism were slyly flirting in the wings. Even before that.

The metamorphosis began when various councils and church associations decided it was time to band together in order to stop the threat of nontraditional religions and to bear down hard and strong on the emerging groups coming strongly into prominence a quarter century ago.

The hysterical symptoms evidenced in those days by the historic churches were evidently substitutes for an unwillingness to face reality or adapt to change. If "traditional religion" had not locked its doors against Mary Baker Eddy, let us say, there would probably be no Church of Christ, Scientist, today, and what we know as "Christian Science" would have been incorporated into the spiritual healing movement which today is being restored to the church-at-large, where it has always belonged.

There would be fewer metaphysical movements today dividing and frequently distorting the religious scene if the church had not ridiculed early metaphysicians like Ernest Holmes and Charles Fillmore and Emmet Fox and Alice Bailey and tagged them as heretics when they presented their views on mystical prayer, mental healing, the art of denial and affirmation, and the value of prosperity thoughts, every last one of which has now been adopted by even the most conservative, fundamentalistic, evangelistic advocate of a present-day approach to faith.

We could say the same about the apocalyptic groups, the Pentecostals, for instance, and the currently accelerating movement of speaking in tongues and the clamor for the baptism of the Holy Spirit, which is now transforming many a staid church parlor into an Upper Room. Time was when the Pentecostals were "foreigners," as offshore as the strangers at our door are today. We strengthened our walls against them and dared them to convince us, if they could, of the measure of their faith. They did. Today we have come full circle to the point where we are proud to admit that "our people" can speak in tongues as well as they, and that we, too, have learned how to handle the Pentecostal fire.

Whoever took Jehovah's Witnesses seriously or the Spiritualists or the Mormons who double their membership every ten years? I must say I did. I took them seriously when I wrote about them in *They Have Found a Faith* and *Faith and My Friends,* and the analogy seems clear to me. The current strangers, most of whom have come from abroad, are being given the same treatment accorded yesterday's emerging groups.

We can psychoanalyze our sectarian selves and arrive at some conclusions about Christianity's failure to convert these strangers before they got the idea of converting us. We can point out, as our social scientists have done, that Christianity abroad has suffered from its divisiveness, its failure to understand native cultures, its collusion with power interests, its hint of spiritual and cultural superiority. We can agree with scholars in the field that Christianity at home has been the victim of our fading morality, our neutralism about plans of salvation, our inflexibility to change, and all the rest. The question remains: now that the strangers are at our door, what shall we do?

Logically we could say: deepen our faith, live the life, hold up the Christ, defend our positions, honor our God. Let us remember that religion is what we theoretically expound, spirituality is what we do with our beliefs in practice.

I come back to my invisible fellowship, the Overchurch. I return to the Cosmic Christ. One way to meet the challenge is to see him in everyman and to silently affirm, as the metaphysical heart of Christianity on the one hand and the power of the Holy Spirit on the other are teaching us, that "the Christ in me salutes the Christ in you!"

Surely, sometimes in our anxiety to get hold of a

182

faith we can intellectually defend and one that will emotionally overwhelm us, we lose touch with the close-at-hand, commonplace things of life. There are times when our concentration on a "spiritual feeling" cuts us off from the kinship with all mankind. I remember how, during *my* Pentecostal days, when I drove through the autumn beauty to go back home to convert my parents, my girlfriend, and all the rest, my missionary zeal blinded me to the silent majesty of the hills, the sight of the river flowing, the sound of singing on the river's bank, and the fellowship of those who had not found what I felt had come to me. Suddenly we were strangers and there were walls.

We can get hung up on a God made in our image. We can become professionally evangelistic. We can turn our righteousness to vanity and our exaggerated faith into an exaggerated suspicion about our fellowmen, failing to see that they have their ecstasy and their own response to love and life which, though it be unlike our own, may be equally meaningful and sincere.

The only answer to the strangers at the door is the answer that the more truly spiritual we are, the more truly compassionate and understanding will we be. The deeper our spiritual convictions, the better can we enjoy the luxury of what others have found. The greater our loyalty to the basic teaching of our churches the more equipped will we be to meet and influence those who have come to influence us. The more we know about their beliefs and their intentions, the more honestly will we be able to evaluate our own.

4

There used to be a strange paradox in religion. It was this: the more a person prided himself on having found the true faith, the more annoyed he was with those who felt they had found the true faith somewhere else. Here, then, were "true faith-ers" kept apart by the very faith each felt he had found. Professing to love God, they could not love others who made the same profession.

Whenever that happened, righteousness became self-righteousness, and in that moment someone suddenly realized that self-righteousness was fully as bad as unrighteousness.

Came the day when that someone went off by himself and got to thinking. He sat in the silence. He walked beside a lake. He stood under the starry sky, thinking. And the moment came when, for the first time in his life, he put himself in the place of the other person.

Teilhard de Chardin once said that the most significant step in the evolution of man took place when "the creature turned the mirror of reflection upon himself." If this is true, then the second greatest event was when man turned the mirror upon his fellowman and discovered himself in him.

When that someone did that, when he realized that the sincerity in others was as meaningful to them as his own sincerity was to him, this did not rob him of his faith—his faith increased. He did not love his spiritual heritage less, he loved it more.

Now he knew that his special convictions blended

with the special convictions held by others, and it dawned on him that all were one. The very last thing he now wanted was for everyone to belong to one church or one faith or one denomination, for he had found unity in plurality, and in it God revealed himself in a far greater way than before.

Yet this someone could not get it out of his mind, much less out of his heart, that somewhere there existed the church of the Spirit, a church invisible without walls. Realizing this, he found others who realized it, too, and for him this was the moment in which the Overchurch was born, and he was seeing the church-at-large as it might conceivably see itself tomorrow.

I rather like these strangers at our door for they are self-challenging, just as all new ideas and ideals prompt us to take a new inventory and work up to our highest good. They have come not so much to convert us or proselytize us, but to remind us that we are at a pivotal, transitional point in religious history, and that now, for the first time, the church—my church, your church—must become more precious as an entity and more real as a collective body of believers in spirit and in truth.

That is why there is no way to meet the challenge unless we proceed beyond "logic" to the creative ground of spiritual understanding. If this is a new way, let us remember it is also a new day.

5

I often come from the quietude of a church other than my own filled with the joy and peace of God. My theological views may by no means have been the same as those of other worshipers. What we found as a common element in our worship was the recognition of something higher and greater than ourselves, the Self beyond self. Who has not discovered this in his own way as he walked from an inspirational service? Knowing what he had found he could only wish with all his heart that others might experience this sense of universal knowing—and perhaps they had.

Surely it must dawn on us that if there were no walls, there would be no need for doors. And I suppose that if we but recognized the spiritual extension of this, and if we could grasp the total meaning of the Cosmic Christ, there would actually be no strangers standing there.

INDEX

187

Index

DATE DUE

GAYLORD   PRINTED IN U.S.A.